THE INSIDER'S
MASTERING MULTIPLE CHOICE

AP U.S. HISTORY 2023 EXAM

by LARRY KRIEGER

THE INSIDER'S
MASTERING MULTIPLE CHOICE
AP U.S. HISTORY 2023 EXAM

by LARRY KRIEGER

ISBN: 978-1-7368182-4-4
An INSIDER TEST PREP publication of Larry Prep LLC
Art Direction & Design by Station16 (Station16 LLC)

For more Insider resources visit
www.InsiderTestPrep.com

TABLE OF CONTENTS

ABOUT THE AUTHOR

Larry Krieger earned his B.A. and M.A.T. from the University of North Carolina at Chapel Hill and his M.A. from Wake Forest University. In a career spanning more than four decades, Mr. Krieger taught in urban, rural, and suburban public high schools in North Carolina and New Jersey. He taught a variety of AP subjects including U.S. History, Art History, European History, and American Government. Mr. Krieger has published popular books in all of these subjects.

Mr. Krieger's AP US History courses were renowned for their energetic presentations, commitment to scholarship, and dedication to helping students achieve high AP exam scores. Over 90 percent of Mr. Krieger's APUSH students scored fives, with the remainder scoring fours. Mr. Krieger has never had an AP student score a one or two.

ACKNOWLEDGEMENTS

Books do not write or publish themselves. They require the work of a number of dedicated and creative peoples.

The typed manuscript must be assembled into an attractive and well-designed book. As always, Station16 more than met this challenge. Brenton played a key leadership role. He developed a distinctive design, offered valuable advice, and as always created an original cover. David proofed each page and Ciara shaped the manuscript into flowing layouts.

PREFACE

Preparing for the 2023 APUSH exam will be a formidable challenge. The current situation has forced schools to use a combination of in-class, distant learning, and hybrid approaches. In addition, an unusually harsh winter has forced many districts to cancel classes. The loss of class time is making it difficult for teachers to complete the required APUSH curriculum.

Given these challenges, my students expressed great concern about how to prepare for the APUSH 2023 multiple-choice questions. The 55 questions in the exam's opening section count 40 percent of the total APUSH score. Reports from students indicate that the multiple-choice questions for the 2021 and 2022 tests were much more challenging than expected. *Mastering APUSH Multiple-Choice Questions* is designed to fulfill its title by providing you with an unprecedented collection of 235 realistic multiple-choice questions.

MY SEARCH FOR AN EFFECTIVE MULTIPLE-CHOICE STRATEGY

My search for an effective multiple-choice strategy began with the APUSH History Course and Exam Description (CED) book. It provides a detailed 237-page presentation of the content and skills that are the focus of the APUSH exam. Topics covered in the CED book are regularly tested. Topics not covered in the CED book will NOT be tested. Unfortunately, many review books and videos ignore this fundamental fact.

APUSH test writers use the CED to generate multiple-choice questions for each exam. We now have an extensive collection of authentic released APUSH multiple-choice questions. My analysis of these questions led me to three key conclusions. First, test writers never write questions asking for specific names, dates, places, and definitions. Second, test writers focus their attention on historic developments, trends, and patterns. And third, test writers are increasingly tying their questions to the texts of each stimulus excerpt.

A BOLD NEW APPROACH

My analysis of the CED book and released APUSH multiple-choice questions led me to create a bold new approach. *Mastering APUSH Multiple-Choice Questions* begins with an Introduction that carefully describes the historical thinking skills tested by multiple-choice questions. Each skill is accompanied by up-to-date question stems.

The book's heart and core is contained in the first nine chapters. Each of these chapters is devoted to one of the nine time periods identified in the CED. The chapters contain 7 prompts and 20 sample multiple-choice questions. Answers and explanations are provided for each question. These prompts and questions focus on key topics that have generated clusters of APUSH questions. Special attention is given to topics from African American and Women's history.

Mastering APUSH Multiple-Choice Questions concludes with a full 55 question Practice Test. This test is followed by answers and explanations designed to provide you with a realistic appraisal of your knowledge and skills. If you find gaps in your knowledge, I recommend you consult the second editions of *The Insider's Fast Review* and *AP US History: A Strategic Review*. These books provide a review of the key content you need to earn high scores on your APUSH exam.

PRACTICE, PRACTICE, PRACTICE

Practice is essential. The APUSH multiple-choice questions will not magically answer themselves. The 82 prompts and 235 questions in this book will help you build your competence and confidence. YOU CAN DO IT!

THE 2023 APUSH EXAM FORMAT

THE EXAM: 3 HOURS AND 15 MINUTES LONG

1. Multiple Choice: 55 questions, 55 minutes, 40 percent of the exam score.
2. Short Answer: 3 questions, 40 minutes, 20 percent of the exam score. The first two short answer questions are mandatory. However, you have a choice between two prompts for the third question.
3. Document-Based Question: 1 question, 60 minutes, 25 percent of the exam score.
4. Long Essay: 1 question, 40 minutes, 15 percent of the exam score. You will have a choice among three prompts for your long essay.

THE APUSH SCALE

Many students assume the APUSH exam contains 100 points and that they need 90 points for a 5, 80 points for a 4, and 70 points for a 3. This common belief is incorrect. The APUSH exam actually contains 140 points. On the 2019 exam students needed 106 points for a 5, 90 points for a 4, and 72 points for a 3. Here is the official APUSH exam score conversion chart for the 2019 APUSH exam:

SCORE RANGE	AP SCORE	MINIMUM PERCENT CORRECT
106–140	5	76 percent
90–105	4	65 percent
72–89	3	52 percent
53–71	2	38 percent
0–52	1	0–37 percent

This chart is not a misprint. You can earn a 3 by correctly answering just 52 percent of the questions, a 4 by answering 65 percent of the questions, and a 5 by answering 76 percent of the questions.

The APUSH scale underscores the importance of the strategic approach used in this book. You do not have to memorize information in a textbook or a series of YouTube videos. Instead, you can achieve a high score by becoming familiar with the developments, trends, and patterns described in this book.

INTRODUCTION
MASTERING MULTIPLE-CHOICE QUESTIONS

BASIC INFORMATION

Number and Importance

Your APUSH exam will begin with a 55-minute section that contains 55 multiple-choice questions. Each question is worth 1 point. Taken together, the 55 multiple-choice questions comprise 40 percent of the 140 points on an APUSH exam. There is no guessing penalty, so be sure to answer each question.

It is important to remember that the APUSH exam scoring scale is much more lenient than the grading systems used by most high schools. In a typical high school, you would have to correctly answer 50 of the 55 multiple-choice questions to earn an A, 49 to earn a B and 39 to earn a C. Relax! On the APUSH exam, correctly answering 29-32 multiple-choice questions will put you on pace to earn a 3! You can earn a 4 by correctly answering 35-37 questions, and a 5 by correctly answering 43-45 questions.

Question Sets

Each multiple-choice question is part of a set located under a stimulus prompt. Most prompts feature a brief passage drawn from an important historic document or written by a professional historian. Political cartoons, graphs, and maps can also serve as prompts.

Recent APUSH exams have contained 17-19 prompts. These prompts generate sets of 2–4 multiple-choice questions. On recent exams, most prompts have been followed by 3 questions.

CONTENT AND REASONING SKILLS

Big-Picture Content

More good news! The multiple-choice questions are not designed to test your ability to recall information from a long list of facts. APUSH test writers will not ask you to remember an obscure fact, a specific date or a remote geographic location.

So what will test writers expect you to know? Multiple-choice questions focus on big-picture content. Test writers craft questions that ask you to demonstrate your understanding of the causes and consequences of important historic trends and influential ideas. For example, a typical test question might ask you to connect the decline of manufacturing employment from 1980 to 2010 with a simultaneous decline in union membership.

Essential Historical Reasoning Skills

Historians do more than study big-picture trends and ideas. As part of their research, they strive to apply historical ways of thinking to the documentary evidence. The APUSH test committee has identified five key historical reasoning skills they deem important: contextualization, causation, continuity and change over time, comparison, and analysis of primary and secondary sources. Each multiple-choice question is designed to test your ability to apply one of these skills to a source document.

1. Contextualization

Historical events do not occur in a vacuum. Contextualization is the ability to connect historical events to a broader setting. Here are 5 frequently used contextual questions. Note that each question asks you to link the prompt to important contemporary developments.

- The excerpt best reflects which of the following?
- Which of the following historical contexts does the image best reflect?
- Which of the following most directly contributes to the sentiments expressed in the excerpt?

- The ideas expressed in the excerpt are most closely connected with which of the following broader historic developments?
- The excerpt can be best understood within the context of which of the following developments?

Contextual questions typically comprise about one-third of the 55 multiple-choice questions on an APUSH exam.

2. Causation

Historians take great pride in their professional curiosity. They strive to identify, analyze, and evaluate the causes and consequences of events and social movements. Historians understand that no single cause can adequately explain a historical episode. Instead, events have multiple causes and effects. Here are 5 frequently used causation questions:

- Which of the following most directly contributed to the conflict referenced in the excerpt?
- Which of the following most directly led to the change described in the excerpt?
- Which of the following was a widespread effect of the market revolution?
- The ideas described in the excerpt contributed most directly to which of the following?
- The opinion excerpted had the effect of…

Causation questions typically comprise about 30 percent of the 55 multiple-choice questions on an APUSH exam.

3. Continuity and Change over Time

Humans live a relatively short time. In contrast, ideas and institutions can endure for centuries. As a result, all periods of American history exhibit some degree of continuity. However, historians also recognize that powerful social forces can produce momentous changes. Historians thus attempt to identify, analyze, and evaluate the dynamics of historical continuity and change over time. Here are 5 frequently used continuity and change over time questions:

- Which of the following was an important continuity in immigration life throughout the 19th century?
- Which of the following best reflects a continuation of the process described in the excerpt?
- Which of the following events best represents continuity of the sentiment expressed by President Washington in his Farewell Address?
- Which of the following best represents a logical extension of the ideas expressed in the excerpt?
- Arguments similar to those expressed in the excerpt were later employed to justify which of the following?

Continuity and change over time typically comprises about 12 percent of the 55 multiple-choice questions on an APUSH exam.

4. Comparison

Historians recognize that history does not repeat itself. However, as the novelist and social critic Mark Twain observed, "History doesn't repeat itself but it does rhyme." APUSH comparison questions ask students to look for those historic rhymes by comparing related historical developments and processes that occur across time or in different societies. Here are 5 frequently used comparison questions:

- Which of the following developments from the 1900s emerged from ideas most similar to those in the excerpt?
- The conflict described in the excerpt is most similar to conflict in which other period?
- Populism, as described in the excerpt, has the most in common with which of the following later domestic reform movements?
- Which of the following later trends was most similar to the pattern described in the excerpt?
- The policies described in the excerpt were most similar to which of the following later developments?

Comparison questions typically comprise about 12 percent of the 55 multiple-choice questions on an APUSH exam.

5. Analysis of Primary and Secondary Sources

Historians make an important distinction between primary and secondary sources. A primary source is a document, speech, or other type of evidence written or produced during the time under study. For example, Carl Schurz's *Report on the Condition of the South* is a primary source description of the South immediately after the Civil War. In contrast, a secondary source provides an interpretation or analysis of primary sources. Secondary sources are thus one-step removed from the original event. For example, Kenneth Stampp's *The Era of Reconstruction, 1865 – 1877* is a secondary source interpretation published a century after the Civil War.

The multiple-choice section of the APUSH exam utilizes a variety of prompts drawn from primary and secondary sources. Here are 5 frequently used questions that test your ability to analyze primary and secondary sources:

- The excerpt most directly expresses a political perspective that…
- Which of the following most directly contradicted the principle established in the opinion excerpted?
- Which of the following could be used to argue against the claims made in the excerpt?
- Which of the following could best be used as evidence to support the argument in the excerpt that…
- People who disagreed with the policies expressed in the excerpt would most likely argue that the government should…

Analyzing primary and secondary source questions typically comprise about 12 percent of the 55 multiple-choice questions on an APUSH exam.

ANSWERING MULTIPLE-CHOICE QUESTIONS

Step 1 – Read the Source Line

Most students begin by carefully reading the passage. Resist this temptation. Instead, begin by focusing on the information in the source line at the end of the passage. Although it is short, the source line provides valuable contextual information.

The information contained in the source line can often enable you to answer many questions without first reading the passage. For example, closely examine the following source line:

Bartolome' de Las Casas, *A Short Account of the Destruction of the Indies*, 1552.

What comes to your mind when you think of Bartolome' de Las Casas? Hopefully, you will recall from Unit 1 that Las Casas was an outspoken critic of the *encomienda* system. The Spanish used this labor system to force Native Americans to harvest sugar cane on West Indian plantations. This cruel system combined with epidemic diseases to decimate the Native American population in this region. As a result, the Spanish began to import enslaved Africans.

Now take a look at the questions. Your knowledge of Las Casas and the *encomienda* system may enable you to answer one or more of the questions! If so, this will save you time and mental energy.

Step 2 – Read the Passage

The passage is called a stimulus for a reason. Don't overanalyze the passage. Instead, read the excerpt and note how the author uses key phrases and evidence to support a main idea. For example, in his speech entitled "The Conquest of Mexico," John C. Calhoun adamantly declared, "Ours, sir, is the Government of a white race." This key idea leads to the logical conclusion that Calhoun would endorse proslavery arguments.

Step 3 – Use the Process of Elimination

Many times your knowledge of the topic will enable you to quickly spot the correct answer. However, there are questions in which the correct answer will not jump out and say, "Here I am!" When this happens, don't panic! APUSH wrong answers are not designed to be tricky. Instead, they fall into three easily identifiable categories.

First and foremost, many answer choices can be eliminated because they are factually incorrect. For example, Lincoln's main purpose in his Gettysburg Address was not to support racial equality. Similarly, Andrew Carnegie's main purpose in his essay on "Wealth" was not to advocate using federal power to redistribute wealth.

Second, many answer choices are true statements that are chronologically out of place. For example, Marcus Garvey's views on black pride were not influenced by Truman's decision to integrate the armed forces. Similarly, President Kennedy's 1963 speech at the Berlin Wall was not influenced by Richard Nixon's 1972 strategy of *détente*.

And finally, many answer choices contain accurate information that is unrelated to the question. For example, Rachel Carson's *Silent Spring* was unrelated to the growing number of Baby Boomers enrolled in college. Similarly, Phyllis Schlafly's argument against the Equal Right Amendment (ERA) was not related to the growing influence of computers.

CHAPTER 1
PERIOD 1
1491 – 1607

PROMPT 1

Questions 1 - 3 refer to the excerpt below:

We are informed that because of the...liberty enjoyed by the said Indians, they avoid contact...with the Spaniards to such an extent that they will not even work for wages, but wander about idle, and cannot be had by the Christians to convert to the Holy Catholic Faith...I command you, our said Governor...you will compel and force the said Indians to associate with the Christians...and to work on their buildings...and mine the gold...and to till the fields and produce food for the Christians...This the Indians shall perform as free people, which they are, and not as slaves.

Instructions from the Spanish Crown to the governor of Hispaniola, 1503

1. The instructions in this excerpt most clearly provide evidence for which of the following?

   A.   The beginning of deadly epidemics that devastated native populations
   B.   The beginning of joint-stock companies to develop gold and silver mines
   C.   The beginning of competition between Spain and France for control of the New World
   D.   The beginning of the *encomienda* system that developed in New Spain

2. Which type of enterprise originally dominated economic activity in Hispaniola?

   A.   Tobacco plantations
   B.   Sugar plantations
   C.   Shipbuilding and fishing
   D.   Textile factories

3. Which of the following was a direct consequence of the widespread death of Native Americans in the West Indies?

   A.   The migration of English Puritans to the West Indies
   B.   The Spanish decision to shift from a feudal to a capitalist economy
   C.   The forcible importation of enslaved people from West Africa
   D.   The decision by Spain to abandon the West Indies and focus instead of conquering Mexico and Peru

PROMPT 2

Questions 4 – 6 refer to the excerpt below:

We…made signs unto them, that we wished them no evil: and as a sign thereof two of our men ventured to go on land to them, and carry them knives with other iron wares, and a red hat to give unto their captain. Which when they saw, they also came on land, and brought some of their skins, and so began to deal with us, seeming to be very glad to have our iron ware and other things…

We sailed up-river and today we reached the village of Stadacona…the chief threw a large feast for everyone. We managed to trade some of our products for some food and gold…We left our ship in the harbor of Stadacona and we set sail with a smaller ship up river. I'm anxious to see what lies ahead. Every day we are getting deeper and deeper inside the continent which increases my curiosity.

Jacques Cartier, Diary entries from his voyages to Canada in 1534 and 1535

4. The pattern of trade described in the excerpt most directly foreshadowed

    A.   the beginning of the fur trade.
    B.   the rise of the trans-Atlantic slave trade.
    C.   the creation of the encomienda labor system.
    D.   the rise of the trans-Atlantic slave trade.

5. Which of the following was a primary feature of social relations in New France?

    A.   The development of an elaborate caste system
    B.   The arrival of a large migration of French settlers
    C.   The development of cooperative relations between French settlers and native tribes
    D.   The emergence of a wealthy planter elite

6. Native Americans in New France most commonly responded to the changes described in this excerpt by

    A.   embracing French religious and agricultural practices.
    B.   becoming pacifists who refused to bear arms.
    C.   adopting French political institutions.
    D.   adopting French material goods while attempting to preserve their own cultural autonomy.

PROMPT 3

Questions 7 – 9 refer to the excerpt below:

Colonial societies did diverge from their mother countries – but in a more complex and radical manner than imagined within the narrow field of vision once traditional to colonial history. The biggest difference was the unprecedented mixing of radically diverse peoples – African, European, and Indian – under circumstances stressful to all. The colonial intermingling of peoples – and of microbes, plants, and animals from different continents – was unparalleled in speed and volume in global history. Everyone had to adapt to a dramatic new world wrought by those combinations.

Alan Taylor, historian, *American Colonies,* **2001**

7. The "intermingling" described by Taylor most directly illustrates which of the following major historic trends in the Atlantic world?

   A.   The spread of maize agriculture across North America
   B.   The phenomenon known as the Columbian Exchange
   C.   The rise of the trans-Atlantic slave trade
   D.   The increasing conflict among European powers over strategic New World trade routes

8. Which of the following was an example of the "dramatic new world" referenced in the excerpt?

   A.   The consolidation of Aztec power in Mexico
   B.   The dramatic increase in population among Native American societies
   C.   The growing spirit of cooperation among Catholic and Protestant countries
   D.   The improved diet, population growth, and economic prosperity in many parts of Europe

9. The Spanish most differed from the English in relations with American Indians in that the Spanish

   A.   rarely intermarried with American Indians.
   B.   rarely used enslaved laborers.
   C.   accepted the religious beliefs of American Indians.
   D.   developed a racially mixed population of European settlers, Native Americans, and Africans.

PROMPT 4

Questions 10 – 12 refer to the excerpt below:

The Spanish have a perfect right to rule these barbarians of the New World and the adjacent islands, who in prudence, skill, virtues, and humanity, are as inferior to the Spanish as children to adults, or women to men… You surely do not expect me to recall at length the prudence and talents of the Spanish… Compare then, our gifts of prudence, talent, magnanimity, temperance, humanity, and religion with those possessed by these half-men, in whom you will barely find the vestiges of humanity, who not only do not possess any learning at all…nor do they have written laws, but barbarian institutions and customs… Therefore, if you wish to reduce them, I do not say to our domination, but to a servitude a little less harsh, it will not be difficult for them to change their masters, and instead of the ones they had, who were barbarous and impious and inhuman, to accept the Christians, cultivators of human virtues and the true faith.

Juan Gines de Sepulveda, *The Second Democrates*, **1547**

10.   Sepulveda's description of Native Americans as "barbarians" best reflects which of the following?

   A.   Assumptions about the superiority of Spanish culture
   B.   Concerns about the possible appeal of New World religious beliefs
   C.   Curiosity about the symbols used in Mayan art
   D.   Worries about the dangers of New World microbes

11.   Which of the following most directly contradicted the argument presented in the excerpt?

   A.   Translations of Mayan works of literature and history
   B.   The discovery of the Fountain of Youth in Florida
   C.   The discovery of the fabled Seven Cities of Gold
   D.   Descriptions of the Aztec capital of Tenochtitlan

12.   Which of the following best describes the goal of Spanish policy in the New World?

   A.   The use of economic incentives to promote commerce and trade
   B.   The use of negotiations to reduce tensions and create alliances
   C.   The use of military power to dominate, control, and exploit
   D.   The use of religion to inspire humanist values

PROMPT 5

Questions 13 – 15 refer to the excerpt below:

For God's sake and man's faith in him, is this the way to impose the yoke of Christ on Christian men? Is this the way to remove wild barbarism from the minds of barbarians?.... The Indian race is not that barbaric, nor are they dull witted or stupid, but they are easy to teach and very talented in learning all the liberal arts, and very ready to accept, honor, and observe the Christian religion…. The Indians are our brothers, and Christ has given his life for them. Why, then, do we persecute them with such inhuman savagery when they do not deserve such treatment?

Bartolome' de Las Casas, *Thirty Very Judicial Propositions*, **1552**

13.   Which of the following is an example of the "inhuman savagery" referenced in the excerpt?

   A.   The use of the encomienda system to organize and exploit Native American labor
   B.   The impressment of Native American sailors onto Spanish ships
   C.   The brutal suppression of pirate raids on Spanish treasure fleets
   D.   The use of forced labor to restore the Aztec's Great Temple

14.   The excerpt implies that the Spanish conquest

   A.   created a thriving economy based upon agricultural surpluses.
   B.   invited an effective Native American resistance movement.
   C.   betrayed the core values of Catholicism.
   D.   spread tobacco cultivation throughout the Caribbean.

15.   The excerpt is best understood in the context of

   A.   Spain's campaign to debunk the "Black Legend" of its brutal treatment of Native Americans.
   B.   a growing campaign to abolish the African slave trade.
   C.   efforts to promote greater religious toleration.
   D.   a debate inside Spain to determine laws and regulations to govern its treatment of Native Americans.

PROMPT 6

Questions 16 – 18 refer to the image below:

The Native American village of Secotan located along the Pamlico River in present-day eastern North Carolina, line engraving by Theodor de Bry, 1590, made from a watercolor by John White.

Library of Congress Rare Book and Special Collection Division.

Questions 16 – 18 refer to the previous image:

16. The image best serves as evidence that Native Americans living along the Eastern Seaboard

   A. developed complex economies based upon the cultivation of tobacco as a cash crop.
   B. developed permanent agrarian settlements.
   C. depended upon horses and iron tools obtained from French traders.
   D. built fortified villages to defend against raids from hostile tribes.

17. Which of the following best describes the effect of images like the one in this excerpt?

   A. They encouraged the English and French to continue searching for a northwest passage to Asia
   B. They sparked interest in finding rich cities like the ones built by the Aztecs and Inca
   C. They convinced English settlers to avoid the harsh realities of life in North America
   D. They influenced the formation of joint-stock companies to invest in founding a North American colony

18. Maize and other New World crops directly influenced Europe by

   A. spreading New World diseases across Europe.
   B. fostering conflict between England, France, and Spain over access to food supplies.
   C. contributing to widespread inflation that began in Spain and spread across Europe.
   D. contributing to the gradual shift of European economies from feudalism to commercial capitalism.

PROMPT 7

Questions 19 – 20 refer to the excerpt below:

Sir, Your Highness [of Portugal] should know how our Kingdom is being lost in so many ways…. This is caused by the excessive freedom given by your agents and officials to the men and merchants who are allowed to come to this Kingdom to set up shops with goods and many things which have been prohibited by us, and which they spread throughout our Kingdoms…in such an abundance that many of our vassals, whom we had in obedience, do not comply because they have the things in greater abundance than we ourselves… it is doing great harm…[to] the security and peace of our Kingdoms….

The mentioned merchants are taking every day our natives, sons of the land and sons our noblemen and vassals and our relatives, because the thieves and men of bad conscience grab them wishing to have the things and wares of this Kingdom which they are ambitious of; they grab them and get them to be sold, and so great, Sir, is the corruption and licentiousness that our country is being completely depopulated.

Letter from King Nzinga Mbemba (Alfonso I) of Kongo to King John III of Portugal, 1526

19. Which of the following most directly shaped the problems described in this excerpt?

  A. The growing importance of Caribbean sugar plantations
  B. The growing importance of Spanish intermarriage with Native Americans
  C. The growing importance of Portuguese Caribbean colonies
  D. The growing importance of French industrial goods

20. The issue highlighted in this excerpt marked the beginning of which of the following long-term trends?

  A. The scaling back of the Portuguese presence in West Africa
  B. The susceptibility of enslaved populations to New World diseases
  C. The emergence of a more industrial economy in the Portuguese New World colonies
  D. The replacement of indigenous labor and indentured servants by enslaved Africans in New World colonies

ANSWERS AND EXPLANATIONS

1. **(D)** The instructions from the Spanish Crown led to the creation of the encomienda system. An encomienda was a license granted to local officials to command and organize the labor of native peoples in a specified area. The encomienda system began in Hispaniola and then spread to Mexico.

2. **(B)** The Spanish quickly discovered that their sugarcane cuttings thrived in Hispaniola's subtropical climate. By 1516, Spanish sugar planters began to export profitable cargoes of sugar to Europe.

3. **(C)** The sudden death of Native American laborers forced Spanish sugar planters to make a fateful decision. Determined to find a large labor force, they began to import large numbers of enslaved Africans to replace the dwindling indigenous population.

4. **(A)** The fur trade became the essential foundation of the New France economy. New France settlers did not cultivate tobacco, create an encomienda labor system, or play a meaningful role in the trans-Atlantic slave trade.

5. **(C)** New France fur trappers lived and worked in scattered trading posts. As a result, they generally avoided conflicts with Native Americans over land and resources.

6. **(D)** Native Americans and the French had divergent religious world views. Nonetheless, since the French did not try to impose Spanish-style missions, Native Americans followed a policy of adopting French metal tools and weapons, while at the same time trying to preserve their own cultural identity.

7. **(B)** The Columbian Exchange refers to the exchange or "intermingling" of microbes, plants, animals, and peoples from Europe, Africa, and the New World.

8. **(D)** The Columbian Exchange affected the New World, West Africa, and Europe in different ways. While it had a devastating impact upon Native America and West Africans, it had a positive impact upon European society by increasing agricultural yields and improving diets thus stimulating population growth and economic prosperity.

9. (D) The Spanish developed a caste system that incorporated and carefully defined the status of a diverse population of Europeans, Africans, and Natve Americans.

10. (A) Like other Spaniards, Sepulveda did not question the superiority of either the Catholic faith or the Spanish artistic and literary achievements.

11. (D) Cortes and other conquistadores wrote detailed descriptions praising Tenochtitlan's busy markets, impressive stone buildings, and lavish royal palaces.

12. (C) The Spanish used their superior iron weapons to successfully topple the Aztec empire.

13. (A) The "inhuman savagery" of the encomienda system appalled Las Casas. He denounced Spanish planters who cruelly exploited defenseless Native Americans.

14. (C) Las Casas criticized the Spanish for ignoring the fundamental Christian tenet that all people are brothers.

15. (D) The Spanish did not attempt to abolish the African slave trade, promote greater religious toleration, or conceal the brutal treatment of Native Americans on their sugar plantations. The defense of Native Americans in this excerpt was part of an ongoing debate in Spain over the empire's colonial policies.

16. (B) The cultivated fields and buildings provide visual evidence that Secotan was a permanent agrarian settlement. It is interesting to note that Secotan did not have walls or other defensive fortifications.

17. (D) The image of Secotan conveyed both peace and prosperity. This encouraged investors to form joint-stock companies to exploit North America's abundant natural resources.

18.   (D) Maize, potatoes, and other nutritious New World crops enriched the European diet, promoted population growth, and stimulated trade and thus commercial capitalism.

19.   (A) The rising economic importance of Caribbean sugar plantations created a growing demand for enslaved African laborers. Although the Portuguese had an important economic presence in Brazil, they had little presence in the Caribbean.

20.   (D) Both Native Americans and indentured servants failed to meet the insatiable demand for labor on New World plantations. This fueled the growth of the trans-Atlantic slave trade.

CHAPTER 2
PERIOD 2
1607 – 1754

Importance: Period 2 generates 6 – 8 percent of the total points on an APUSH exam.

Key Events: The founding of Jamestown, King Philip's War, Bacon's Rebellion, the Atlantic slave trade, and the First Great Awakening are the most frequently tested events from this period of time.

Additional Resources: See Chapter 2 in the 2023 edition of **Fast Review** for a concise summary of key developments, trends, and patterns tested in Period 2.

PROMPT 1

Questions 1 - 3 refer to the excerpt below:

This is to let you understand that I your child am in most heavy case by reason of the country, is such that it causeth much sickness, as the scurvy and the bloody flux and diverse other diseases which maketh the body very poor and weak…I have nothing to comfort me, nor is there nothing to be gotten here but sickness and death, except [in the event] that one had money to layout in some things for profit. But I have nothing at all – no, not a shirt to my back but two rags, nor no clothes but one poor suit, not but one pair of shoes, but one pair of stockings, but one cap…I am not half a quarter so strong as I was in England, and it is for want of victuals; for I do protest unto you that I have eaten more in a day at home than I have allowed me here for a week…

Richard Frethorne, indentured servant working in Virginia, letter to his mother and father, 1623

1. Which of the following contexts most directly shaped the conditions described in the excerpt?

    A. Tensions between tobacco planters and independent farmers
    B. Tensions between tobacco planters and indentured servants
    C. Tensions between Anglican and Puritan settlers
    D. Tensions between English colonists in the Chesapeake and Spanish colonists in the Caribbean

2. Which of the following was a long-term result of the plight of indentured servants?

    A. The development of new trade routes with Spanish colonies
    B. The reduction of tensions with Native Americans
    C. The rapid growth of small compact towns
    D. The replacement of indentured servants with enslaved Africans colonists in the Caribbean

3. The excerpt would be most useful to historians as a source of information about

    A. The rigors of life in early colonial Virginia.
    B. The economic conditions in England during the early 1600s.
    C. The interaction between Virginia settlers and Native Americans.
    D. The role advertising played in persuading men and women to become indentured servants.

PROMPT 2

Questions 4 – 6 refer to the excerpt below:

God requireth not a uniformity of religion to be enacted and enforced in any civil state; which enforced uniformity sooner or later is the greatest occasion of civil war, ravishing of conscience, persecution of Christ Jesus in his servants, and of the hypocrisy and destruction of millions of souls.

Roger Williams, "A Plea for Religious Liberty," 1644

4. The emphasis on religious liberty, which Williams articulated in the 1640s, was most strongly enacted by the

   A. First Amendment.
   B. Second Amendment.
   C. Fourteenth Amendment.
   D. Twentieth Amendment.

5. The excerpt best reflects which of the following developments in Massachusetts Bay in the 1630s?

   A. Religious enthusiasm sparked the beginning of the First Great Awakening
   B. Religious controversies inspired a movement to train more orthodox ministers
   C. Religious intolerance fostered religious tolerance in nearby colonies
   D. Religious disagreements generated calls for renewed efforts to raise the education level of young girls and women

6. Which of the following most directly influenced the point of view in this excerpt?

   A. The founding of Harvard College
   B. The desire to convert Native Americans to Puritanism
   C. The Puritan ideal of founding a Bible Commonwealth
   D. The trial and banishment of religious dissenters

PROMPT 3

Questions 7 – 9 refer to the excerpt below:

By August 1676 when Philip was shot to death near his home in Mount Hope, twenty-five English towns, more than half of all the colonists' settlements in New England, had been ruined and the line of English habitation had been pushed back almost to the coast…Yet the Indian losses were greater…Algonquians who fought the English saw their communities decimated; thousands were killed in the fighting while thousands more died of disease or starvation or were shipped out of the colonies as slaves…It has been the fate of the American frontier to endlessly repeat itself…The same cultural anxieties and land conflicts that drove Indians and colonists to war in 1675 would continue to haunt them after the war had ended.

Jill Lapore, *The Name of War, King Philip's War and the Origins of American Identity*, **1998**

7. The conflict between Native Americans and New England colonists was primarily caused by differing

   A. philosophies of government.
   B. farming strategies.
   C. patterns of trade.
   D. views of the ownership and value of land.

8. Which of the following statements describes the impact of King Philip's War on relations between Native Americans and New England colonists?

   A. The war triggered even more destructive conflicts
   B. Native Americans and colonists restored their once harmonious relationship
   C. Colonists assumed a dominant position throughout New England
   D. Native Americans reformed into powerful local tribes

9. Which of the following historical developments supports Lapore's argument in the excerpt's final two sentences?

   A. White settlers began to respect Native American cultural traditions
   B. Relations between the United States government and American Indians inevitably deteriorated because of disputes over land
   C. Political divisions between the United States government and American Indians arose over the expansion of slavery into the Western territories
   D. The market revolution shifted public attention from Indian affairs

PROMPT 4

Questions 10 – 12 refer to the excerpt below:

Let us trace…[the] men in authority and favor to whose hands the dispensation of the country's wealth has been committed. Let us observe the sudden rise of their estates…[compared] with the quality in which they first entered this country. Let us consider their sudden advancement. And let us also consider whether any public work for our safety and defense or for the advancement and propagation of trade, liberal arts or sciences is in any [way] adequate to our vast charge. Now let us compare these things together and see what sponges have sucked up the public treasure and whether it has not been privately contrived away by unworthy favorites and juggling parasites whose tottering fortunes have been repaired and supported at the public charge.

Nathaniel Bacon, "Manifesto," 1676

10.   Which of the following most directly contributed to the complaints that motivated this excerpt?

   A.   The growing disparity between the influence of Virginia and Pennsylvania in colonial affairs
   B.   The growing disparity between the power of the Native American tribes and Tidewater planters
   C.   The growing disparity between the fortunes of the Tidewater gentry and former indentured servants
   D.   The growing disparity between the wealth of England and other colonial empires

11.   Which of the following would most likely have supported the opinions expressed in the excerpt at the time it was written?

   A.   Tidewater tobacco planters
   B.   Royal officials in Virginia
   C.   Members of Parliament in London
   D.   Independent farmers living on Virginia's frontier

12.   Bacon most likely wrote his "Manifesto" in order to

   A.   justify his opposition to Virginia's royal officials.
   B.   promote an alliance between colonists in Virginia and colonists in South Carolina.
   C.   endorse renewed efforts to find gold and promote the fur trade.
   D.   propose a treaty of reconciliation with Native American tribes.

PROMPT 5

Questions 13 – 15 refer to the excerpt below:

In 1739 arrived among us from Ireland the Reverend Mr. [George] Whitefield, who made himself remarkable there as an itinerant preacher. He was at first permitted to preach in some of our churches; but the clergy, taking a dislike to him, soon refused him their pulpits, and he was obliged to preach in the fields. The multitudes of all sects and denominations that attended his sermons were enormous….It was wonderful to see the change soon made in the manners of our inhabitants. From being thoughtless or indifferent about religion, it seemed as if all the world were growing religious, so that one could not walk thro' the town in an evening without hearing psalms in different families of every street.

Benjamin Franklin, description of a religious revival held in 1739,
The Autobiography of Benjamin Franklin

13.   Which of the following would most likely have opposed the style and setting of the revival meeting described in this excerpt?

A.   Itinerant ministers

B.   Old Light ministers

C.   Independent farmers

D.   Enslaved Africans

14.   Which of the following broader contexts most directly contributed to the success of revivals such as the one described in this excerpt?

A.   The widespread circulation of printed materials in the colonies

B.   The widespread support for the ideology of republican motherhood

C.   The widespread calls for a new economic relationship with Great Britain

D.   The widespread movement to abolish the trans-Atlantic slave trade

15.   Which of the following occurred most directly as a result of the religious movement described in this excerpt?

A.   The growth of Enlightenment rationalism

B.   The rapid expansion of colonial commerce

C.   The continued westward migration of settlers

D.   The emergence of numerous Dissenting churches

PROMPT 6

Questions 16 – 17 refer to the excerpt below:

My Fathers and Brethren, this is never to be forgotten that New England is originally a plantation of Religion, not a Plantation of Trade. Let merchants and such as are increasing Cent per Cent remember this…that worldly gain was not the end and designe of the people of New England, but Religion.

John Higginson, "The Cause of God and His People in New England," 1662

16.   The author of this excerpt would most likely agree that the original Puritan mission was to

A.   create a new society that would champion religious toleration.
B.   create a model society that would serve as an ideal Christian commonwealth.
C.   create an egalitarian society that would equitably distribute property and power.
D.   create a free society that opposed indentured servitude and slavery.

17.   Higginson's argument in the passage is best explained in the context of

A.   the destruction caused by King Philip's War.
B.   the religious controversy caused by the trial of Anne Hutchinson.
C.   the growing prosperity of coastal fishermen and shipbuilders.
D.   the decision to found Harvard College.

PROMPT 7

Questions 18 – 20 refer to the excerpt below:

Five of our number in the passage dy'd,

Who were cast into the ocean wide,

And, after sailing seven weeks and more,

We, at Virginia all were put ashore.

Into the field I next did go,

Among tobacco plants all day to hoe,

At day break in the morn our work begun,

And lasted till the setting of the sun.

My fellow slaves were five transports more,

With eighteen Negroes which is twenty four,

Besides four transport women in the house,

To wait upon his daughter and his spouse.

We and the Negroes both alike did fare,

Of work and food we had an equal share…

My countrymen, take warning e'er too late,

Lest you shou'd share my unhappy fate.

**James Revel, "A Poor Unhappy Transported Felon's Sorrowful
Account of His Fourteen Years' Transportation at Virginia, in America," 1680**

Questions 18 – 20 refer to the previous excerpt:

18.   The excerpt was most likely intended to do which of the following?

   A.   Address the need to import more African slaves into the Virginia colony
   B.   Alleviate concerns about the difficulties faced by indentured servants
   C.   Raise questions about the efficacy of becoming an indentured servant
   D.   Question the Virginia colony's growing dependence upon cultivating tobacco as a cash crop

19.   The excerpt serves as evidence of which of the following trends during the last quarter of the seventeenth century?

   A.   The increasing reliance on the labor of indentured servants
   B.   The flourishing trade between Virginia and the West Indies
   C.   The continuing conflict between the Virginia colonists and the Powhatan Confederacy
   D.   The growing use of enslaved Africans on Virginia tobacco plantations

20.   Based on the excerpt, Revel would have most closely identified with

   A.   A rebellion by slaves such as the Stono Rebellion.
   B.   A rebellion by frustrated small farmers such as Bacon's Rebellion.
   C.   An uprising by indigenous people as the Pueblo Revolt.
   D.   An uprising by a Native American confederation such as King Philip's War.

ANSWERS AND EXPLANATIONS

1. (B) Richard Frethorne faced desperate living conditions. However, he implies that the situation is much better for those who have "money to layout in some things for profit." The tension between tobacco planters and their exploited indentured servants became an important feature of life in 17th century Virginia.

2. (D) Bacon's Rebellion exposed tensions between Tidewater planters and back country former indentured servants. As planters became wary of their former indentured servants, they turned to enslaved Africans as a more reliable and cost-effective source of labor.

3. (A) This excerpt provides a graphic and poignant insight into the plight of indentured servants at a time when the Jamestown colony tottered on the brink of collapse.

4. (A) The First Amendment codifies Williams's call for religious liberty by stating, "Congress shall make no law respecting an establishment of religion, or prohibiting the free exercise thereof…"

5. (C) The Puritans emphasized religious conformity. Although they came to America for religious freedom, they did not tolerate outspoken dissidents such as Anne Hutchinson and Roger Williams. Ironically, their religious intolerance fostered a tradition of religious tolerance in Rhode Island.

6. (D) At the time Williams wrote "A Plea for Religious Liberty," Puritan authorities had already banished him and Anne Hutchinson for their unorthodox religious and political views. Williams founded the Rhode Island colony where he championed religious toleration, freedom of thought, and the separation of church and state.

7. (D) Tensions quickly arose between Native Americans and New England colonists as the settlers placed relentless pressure on tribal lands and resources. Native Americans viewed land as a common resource that could not be bought or sold. In contrast, the colonists viewed land as a valuable commodity that individuals could buy, sell, and profit from.

8. (C) Although they suffered significant losses, the New England colonists successfully broke the power of the local Native American tribes. The surviving Native peoples now lived on the margins of a land they had once controlled.

9. (B) Treaties between the United States government and American Indians in the post-Civil War West usually lasted a short time before being broken by settlers' incursions onto American Indian reservations. For example, the conflict between the Sioux nation and the United States was primarily driven by differing claims to land.

10. (C) Virginia's former indentured servants enjoyed a brief period of prosperity. However, falling tobacco prices, rising taxes, and dwindling opportunities to purchase fertile land caused mounting levels of frustration and income inequality. These grievances fueled a growing anger directed at Virginia Governor William Berkeley and the wealthy planters he favored.

11. (D) Tidewater tobacco planters and royal officials in Virginia and London all opposed Bacon. In contrast, Bacon successfully voiced the complaints of independent farmers living on Virginia's frontier.

12. (A) Bacon wrote his Manifesto to explain and justify his opposition to Virginia's royal officials. Choices B, C, and D can all be eliminated because they are historically inaccurate.

13. (B) The "Old Light" Puritan ministers continued to deliver long intellectual sermons emphasizing elaborate theological doctrines. They resented Whitefield and other "New Light" ministers who favored spontaneous and impassioned outdoor sermons.

14. (A) Sermons, theological treatises, and copies of the Bible were by far the largest category of material published by colonial printers. Ben Franklin's detailed coverage of Whitefield's sermon helped publicize the evangelist's speaking tour.

15.   (D) The Great Awakening led to divisions within the established Anglican, Congregationalist, and Presbyterian churches. In addition, Baptist and Methodist churches became more popular. The emergence of numerous Dissenting churches created a religiously pluralistic society that supported toleration since no single denomination could impose its will on the others.

16.   (B) The original Puritans had a powerful sense of mission. John Winthrop's famous "City Upon a Hill" sermon expressed the Puritan belief that they had a special pact with God to build a model Christian society.

17.   (C) Higginson's excerpt reflects the decline of religious zeal as the Puritan society grew and became increasingly prosperous.

18.   (C) Revel describes a dangerous voyage followed by endless days of toil. He concludes by warning his countrymen to avoid his "unhappy fate."

19.   (D) Revel notes that Negroes comprised 18 percent of the 24 male workers. Written a few years after Bacon's Rebellion, Revel's poem reflects the growing use of enslaved Africans on Virginia's tobacco plantations.

20.   (B) As an indentured servant, Revel would have probably been sympathetic with members of other exploited groups. However, he would have most likely closely identified with the exploited indentured servants and disenfranchised Englishmen who participated in Bacon's Rebellion.

CHAPTER 3
PERIOD 3
1754 – 1800

Importance: Period 3 generates 10 – 17 percent of the total points on an APUSH exam.

Key Terms: Republicanism, Republican motherhood, Federalists, Anti-Federalists

Key Events: The road to revolution, the weaknesses of the Articles of Confederation, the Constitutional Convention, the debate over ratification, the national bank controversy

Additional Resources: See Chapter 3 in the 2023 edition of **Fast Review** for a concise summary of key developments, trends, and patterns tested in Period 2.

PROMPT 1

Questions 1 - 2 refer to the excerpt below:

The enormity of Britain's victory [in the Seven Years' War] seemed to herald a new world order. "No prince had ever begun his reign by so glorious a war and so generous a peace," Lord Egremont was reported to have said to George III as they looked over the terms of the Peace of Paris. But what would the new world order look like, and how would it be governed?...The Seven Years' War and the empire it brought helped bind English and Scots in a common imperial venture. But in America, it helped drive Britons apart.

Colin G. Calloway, historian, The Scratch of a Pen – 1763 and the *Transformation of North America*, **2006**

1. Which of the following began the process of driving Great Britain and her American colonies apart?

    A.   The increasing divergence between colonial and British culture
    B.   Debates over how Britain's colonies should bear the cost of the Seven Years' War
    C.   Complaints about high tariffs imposed on tobacco exports
    D.   The lack of American representatives in the British Parliament

2. The "new world order" referenced in the excerpt included which of the following features?

    A.   A continuing security threat posed by the French Canadians
    B.   The mass migration of Americans settlers across the Appalachian Mountains
    C.   The return of valuable Caribbean sugar islands to France
    D.   An agreement between the United States and France to relocate Native Americans to lands west of the Mississippi River

PROMPT 2

Questions 3 – 5 refer to the excerpt below:

The hopes of reconciliation, which were fondly entertained by multitudes of honest and well meaning, though weak and mistaken people, have been gradually and, at last, totally extinguished. Time has been given for the whole people maturely to consider the great question of independence, and to ripen their judgment, dissipate their fears, and allure their hopes, by discussing it in newspapers and pamphlets, by debating it in assemblies, conventions, committees of safety and inspection, in town and county meetings, as well as in private conversations, so that the whole people, in every colony of the thirteen, have now adopted it as their own act....

John Adams, Letters of John Adams, Addressed to his Wife, July 3, 1776

3. Adams reference to "the hopes of reconciliation" suggest that

   A.   many Americans had previously supported a compromise between submission to British authority and independence.

   B.   some New England colonies threatened to unite with the French Canadians.

   C.   the inclusion of abolitionism as a goal threatened to disrupt colonial unity.

   D.   political parties actively promoted independence.

4. Which of the following was a key part of the colonial debate about independence?

   A.   The drafting of the United States Constitution

   B.   The issuing of George Washington's Farewell Address

   C.   The publication of the Federalist Papers

   D.   The publication of the pamphlet *Common Sense*

5. Which of the following was an integral part of the colonial consensus supporting independence?

   A.   The concept of hereditary rights

   B.   The widespread belief in Manifest Destiny

   C.   The principle of religious freedom

   D.   The commitment to republican values

PROMPT 3

Questions 6 – 8 refer to the excerpt below:

This enquiry is important, because, although the government reported by the convention does not go to a perfect and entire consolidation, yet it approaches so near to it, that it must, if executed, certainly and infallibly terminate in it. The government is to possess absolute and uncontrollable power, legislative, executive, and judicial, with respect to every object to which it extends....It appears from these articles, that there is no need of any intervention of the state governments, between the Congress and the people, to execute any one power vested in the general government, and that the constitution and laws of every state are nullified and declared void, so far as they are or shall be inconsistent with this constitution, or the laws made in pursuance of it...The government, then, so far as it extends, is a complete one, and not a confederation...

Brutus No. 1. 1787, Brutus is a likely pseudonym of Robert Yates

6. During the constitutional ratification process, Anti-Federalists' concerns, as described in this excerpt, were most directly addressed by an agreement to

   A.   extend voting rights to all white men over the age of 21.
   B.   eliminate the international slave trade.
   C.   incorporate political parties into the Constitution.
   D.   add a Bill of Rights to the Constitution.

7. The excerpt most directly reflects the belief held by many in 1787 that

   A.   a national bank was needed to promote economic growth.
   B.   a stronger central government posed a threat to the independence of state governments.
   C.   the United States should avoid entangling alliances with European powers.
   D.   Native Americans should be moved to lands west of the Appalachian Mountains.

8. In the decades following the ratification of the Constitution, policy debates continued over which issue raised in this excerpt?

   A.   The rapid development of a market economy
   B.   The growing popularity of the idea of Manifest Destiny
   C.   The relationship between national and state governments
   D.   The establishment of the Supreme Court

PROMPT 4

Questions 9 – 11 refer to the excerpt below:

The Congress shall have power to lay and collect taxes, duties, imposts, and excises, to pay the debts and provide for the common defense, and general welfare of the United States, but all duties, imposts and excises shall be uniform throughout the United States....

[And] to make all laws which shall be necessary and proper for carrying into executions the foregoing powers, and all other powers vested by the Constitution in the government of the United States, or in any department or officer thereof.

The United States Constitution, Article One, Section Eight, 1787

9. Which of the following historical contexts does this excerpt best reflect?

    A.   The property damage caused by Shays' Rebellion

    B.   The lack of legal rights granted to women

    C.   The perceived weaknesses of the Articles of Confederation

    D.   The belief that a system of checks and balances would make it difficult for a special interest to dominate the government

10.   Debates over the interpretation of this excerpt most directly contributed to

    A.   increased American participation in trans-Atlantic trade.

    B.   restrictions placed on Federalist policies.

    C.   the formation of a two-party system.

    D.   the economic shift from agriculture to industrial production.

11.   Supporters of the broadest interpretation of this excerpt would have been most likely to support which of the following?

    A.   Clay's American System

    B.   Jefferson's view of states' rights

    C.   Calhoun's doctrine of nullification

    D.   Jackson's veto of the bill to recharter the National Bank

PROMPT 5

Questions 12 – 14 refer to the excerpt below:

The migration or importation of such persons as any of the States now existing shall think proper to admit, shall not be prohibited by the Congress prior to the year one thousand eight hundred and eight, but a tax or duty may be imposed on such importation, not exceeding ten dollars for each person.

Article I, Section 9, United States Constitution, 1787

12. The expression "such persons" was used to mean

   A. Anti-Federalists.
   B. enslaved Africans.
   C. indentured servants.
   D. Loyalists.

13. Which of the following was a reason why northern delegates accepted this provision?

   A. They wanted to collect badly needed revenue
   B. They wanted to let the Supreme Court resolve the issue
   C. They wanted to establish a limited federal government
   D. They wanted to avoid a dispute that could fracture the Constitutional Convention

14. The excerpt most directly provides evidence for which of the following?

   A. The continuing dispute over the meaning of popular sovereignty.
   B. The abolitionist roots of the Republican Party.
   C. The willingness of the delegates to postpone sectional tensions.
   D. The commitment of Northern delegates to profit from the triangular trade.

PROMPT 6

Questions 15 – 17 refer to the excerpt below:

The education of young ladies, in this country, should be conducted upon principles… in some respects different from what it was when we were part of a monarchical empire…The equal share that every citizen has in the liberty, and the possible share he may have in government of our country, make it necessary that our ladies should be qualified to a certain degree, by a peculiar and suitable education, to concur in instructing their sons in the principles of liberty and government.

Benjamin Rush, physician and political leader from Pennsylvania,
Thoughts Upon Female Education, **1787.**

15. The women referred to in this excerpt would have most typically engaged in which of the following activities during the Revolutionary War?

   A. Participating in boycotts of British goods
   B. Forming abolitionist societies
   C. Campaigning for the right to vote
   D. Announcing efforts to promote temperance

16. The concerns expressed by Rush were a response to

   A. the treatment of American Loyalists.
   B. the dispute over the proper treatment of Native American tribes.
   C. the growing sectional tensions between the North and the South.
   D. the discrepancy between the status of women and their role in the new American republic.

17. The opinion expressed in the excerpt would most likely have been held by

   A. a Southern planter.
   B. a Federalist.
   C. an advocate of republican motherhood.
   D. an advocate of religious freedom.

PROMPT 7

Questions 18 – 20 refer to the excerpt below:

Yet definitions of the private came to encompass a covertly political role: that of the republican wife and mother who by her work in the domestic realm allowed her husband to fulfill his responsibilities to the public outside the household, and who carefully raised her children - especially her sons – to be good citizens of the new nation. In such an ideological context, some women found scope for social activism as an extension of their domestic responsibilities; for example, they formed female charitable or religious organizations to aid widows and orphans or support missionary endeavors.

Mary Beth Norton, historian, *Separated By Their Sex***, 2011**

18.   Which of the following best reflects "work in the domestic realm" that women engaged in during the 1790s?

   A.   Enforcing boycotts of British imported goods
   B.   Seeking employment in New England textile mills
   C.   Participating in the urban consumer culture
   D.   Campaigning to reform facilities for the mentally ill

19.   The change described in the excerpt most immediately contributed to which of the following developments?

   A.   Expansion of the settlement house movement
   B.   Opening new academic schools for women
   C.   Increased participation in serving on juries
   D.   Taking a more active role in political parties

20.   Which of the following historical developments during the late 1820s best supports the trend for women to extend their domestic responsibilities by participating in partisan activities?

   A.   Women engaged in protests against the War of 1812
   B.   Women rallied public opposition against the Tariff of Abominations
   C.   Women supported extending the charter of the Second Bank of the United States
   D.   Women actively opposed the Indian Removal Act

ANSWERS AND EXPLANATIONS

1. (B) The high cost of the Seven Years' War left Britain with an enormous national debt. Parliament passed the Stamp Act to raise revenue to help pay for British troops stationed in America. Outraged colonial leaders insisted that only their provincial assemblies had the power to raise taxes.

2. (C) Choices A, B, and D are historically inaccurate. The Treaty of Paris of 1763 ended French power in North America but did return several valuable Caribbean sugar islands to France.

3. (A) Many Americans sought a compromise solution to bridge their differences with Great Britain. For example, the First Continental Congress narrowly defeated Galloway's compromise plan.

4. (D) Thomas Paine published *Common Sense* to persuade the colonies to declare their independence from Great Britain. *Common Sense* became an instant bestseller as people throughout the colonies agreed with Paine's compelling argument for independence.

5. (D) Republicanism is the belief that government should be based upon the consent of the governed. As resistance to British taxes intensified, colonial leaders became more and more committed to republican values.

6. (D) Brutus and other leading Anti-Federalists warned that the proposed new government would possess "absolute and uncontrollable power." The Federalists assuaged this concern by agreeing to add a Bill of Rights to the Constitution.

7. (B) Brutus and other leading Anti-Federalists argued that the Constitution replaced a confederation of relatively independent states with a consolidated federal government.

8. (C) Issues like the national bank, tariffs, and internal improvements sparked contentious debates over the relationship between the national and state governments.

9. (C) The necessary and proper or elastic clause was a response to the perceived limitations of the weak and ineffective Congress established by the Articles of Confederation.

10. (C) Strict constructionists like Thomas Jefferson argued that what the Constitution does not permit, it forbids. In contrast, loose constructionists like Alexander Hamilton argued that what the Constitution does not forbid, it permits. These two contrasting views played an important role in the formation of the Democratic-Republican and Federalist political parties.

11. (A) Proponents of a broad or loose interpretation of the necessary and proper clause supported Clay's American System.

12. (B) The phrase "such persons" was a euphemism for enslaved Africans.

13. (D) Northern delegates recognized that slavery was a contentious issue that could divide the delegates. They therefore reached a compromise based upon their overriding goal of distinguishing the possible from the impossible.

14. (C) The decision to allow the slave trade to continue for another twenty years allowed South Carolina and Georgia to replenish slaves evacuated by the British during the Revolutionary War. The compromise thus postponed sectional tensions over slavery.

15. (A) Led by the Daughters of Liberty, many colonial women supported the Revolutionary War by organizing boycotts of British goods.

16. (D) Despite their emphasis upon liberty and equality, the Framers of the Constitution did not address the issue of women's subordinate legal status.

17.   (C) Advocates of republican motherhood believed women had an important responsibility to become exemplary parents who would raise their children to become virtuous citizens.

18.   (C) Women did not boycott British goods, seek employment in New England textile mills, or campaign for the mentally ill during the 1790s. However, they did actively participate in the urban consumer culture as purchasers of goods such as tea, milk, butter, candles, sheets, coats, and gowns.

19.   (B) Reformers recognized women needed a better education in order to fulfill their role as republican mothers. Led by the New England states, many communities began to open private schools and academies devoted to improving educational opportunities for American women.

20.   (D) By the late 1820s, forming female charitable or religious organizations no longer proved adequate for women who wanted to have a more direct impact on political matters of concern to the nation as a whole. As a result, women activists became involved in partisan activities such as opposition to Indian removal.

CHAPTER 4
PERIOD 4
1800 – 1848

Importance: Period 45 generates 10 – 17 percent of the total points on an APUSH exam.

Key Terms: American System, Jacksonian democracy, nullification, market revolution, Second Great Awakening, cult of domesticity

Key Events: Rise of political parties, market revolution, Jacksonian democracy, Second Great Awakening, Seneca Falls Convention

Additional Resources: See Chapter 4 in the 2023 edition of **Fast Review** for a concise summary of key developments, trends, and patterns tested in Period 4.

PROMPT 1

Questions 1 - 3 refer to the excerpt below:

The Government of the Union, though limited in its powers, is supreme within its sphere of action, and its laws, when made in pursuance of the Constitution, form the supreme law of the land.

If the end be legitimate, and within the scope of the Constitution, all the means which are appropriate, which are plainly adapted to that end, and which are not prohibited, may constitutionally be employed to carry it into effect...

The States have no power, by taxation or otherwise, to retard, impede, burden, or in any manner control the operations of the constitutional laws enacted by Congress to carry into effect the powers vested in the national Government.

United States Supreme Court, *McCulloch v. Maryland,* **1819**

1. In *McCulloch v. Maryland,* the Supreme Court established which of the following principles?
   A.   The federal government alone may levy taxes
   B.   The federal Bill of Rights places no limitations on the states
   C.   The supremacy of the national government over the states
   D.   The powers of the federal government cannot go beyond those enumerated by the Constitution

2. Which of the following most directly disputed the principle established in *McCulloch v. Maryland?*
   A.   The passage of the Northwest Ordinance of 1787
   B.   The use of party conventions to nominate presidential candidates
   C.   The argument presented in the South Carolina Exposition and Protest
   D.   The demands approved by the Seneca Falls Convention

3. *McCulloch v. Maryland* and *Gibbons v. Ogden* are similar Supreme Court decisions in that both cases
   A.   established a constitutional right to privacy.
   B.   strengthened the power of the national government.
   C.   protected the reserved powers of state governments.
   D.   established the principle that the judicial branch cannot intervene in political disputes between the President and Congress.

PROMPT 2

Questions 4 – 6 refer to the excerpt below:

This momentous question, like a fire bell in the night, awakened and filled me with terror. I considered it at once as the knell of the Union. It is hushed indeed for the moment. But this is a reprieve only, not a final sentence. A geographical line, coinciding with a marked principle, moral and political, once conceived and held up to the angry passions of men, will never be obliterated and every new irritation will mark it deeper and deeper.

Thomas Jefferson, Letter to John Holmes, April 22, 1820

4. The excerpt most directly responds to which "momentous question"?

   A.   The passage of the Missouri Compromise
   B.   The passage of the Tariff of Abominations
   C.   The passage of the Indian Removal Act
   D.   The passage of the Wilmot Proviso

5. The "geographical line" referenced in the excerpt refers to

   A.   the line excluding slavery from new European colonies in the Western Hemisphere.
   B.   the line excluding slavery from all territories north of the Ohio River and east of the Mississippi River.
   C.   the line excluding slavery from most of the Louisiana Territory.
   D.   the line excluding slavery from all territories ceded to the United States in the Treaty of Guadalupe Hidalgo.

6. Which of the following historical developments provides the best evidence in support of Jefferson's warning about "the angry passions of men"?

   A.   The Trail of Tears
   B.   Bleeding Kansas
   C.   The Mexican-American War
   D.   A continuous series of slave revolts

PROMPT 3

Questions 7 – 9 refer to the excerpt below:

America, in the assembly of nations, since her admission among them, has invariably, though often fruitlessly, held forth to them the hand of honest friendship, of equal freedom, of generous reciprocity. She has uniformly spoken among them, though often to heedless, and disdainful ears, the language of equal liberty, of equal justice, and of equal rights. She has, in the lapse of nearly half a century, without single exception, respected the independence of other nations while asserting and maintaining her own…But she goes not abroad, in search of monsters to destroy. She is the well-wisher to the freedom and independence of all. She is the champion and vindicator of her own. She will command the general cause by the countenance of her voice, and the sympathy of her example.

John Quincy Adams, Fourth of July Address, 1821

7. The views expressed in the excerpt contributed most directly to

    A.   the outbreak of rebellions in Haiti and Latin America.
    B.   the elimination of the international slave trade.
    C.   the desire to settle new territories controlled by American Indians.
    D.   the formulation of what became known as the Monroe Doctrine.

8. Which of the following most directly contradicted the principles declared in the opinion excerpted?

    A.   Washington's Neutrality Proclamation
    B.   The Non-Intercourse Act
    C.   The Battle of Tippecanoe
    D.   The Louisiana Purchase

9. The ideas expressed in Adams's address most strongly influenced which United States foreign policy decision in the twentieth century?

    A.   America's refusal to join the League of Nations
    B.   America's decision to form the NATO alliance
    C.   America's decision to suppress the Philippine Insurrection
    D.   America's campaign to suppress aliens and radicals during the Red Scare

PROMPT 4

Questions 10 – 11 refer to the excerpt below:

In Park Street Church, on the Fourth of July, 1829, in an address on slavery, I unreflectingly assented to the popular but pernicious doctrine of gradual abolition. I seize this opportunity to make a full and unequivocal recantation, and thus publicly to ask pardon of my God, of my country, and of my brethren the poor slaves, for having uttered a sentiment so full of timidity, injustice, and absurdity....On the subject of slavery...I will be as harsh as truth, and as uncompromising as justice. On this subject I do not wish to think, or speak, or write, with moderation. No! No!...I am in earnest – I will not equivocate – I will not excuse – I will not retreat a single inch – AND I WILL BE HEARD.

William Lloyd Garrison, first issue of abolitionist newspaper, *The Liberator,*
January 1, 1831

10. Which of the following most directly contributed to the argument advanced in this excerpt?

   A. The ongoing success of the American Colonization Society.
   B. The ongoing campaign to pass the Thirteenth Amendment.
   C. The ongoing reform movements inspired by the Second Great Awakening.
   D. The ongoing market revolution in transportation and communication.

11. Which of the following would most likely have supported the position taken in the excerpt at the time it was written?

   A. Southern Redeemers
   B. Populist Party activists
   C. Republican Party politicians
   D. Advocates for women's rights

PROMPT 5

Questions 12 – 13 refer to the excerpt below:

As an instance of the rapid manner in which travelers get along, I may instance Mrs. Lloyd's trip to Richmond in Virginia. She left Philadelphia at six o'clock A.M.....and arrived in the evening of the second day from Philadelphia at the city of Richmond thus traversing without fatigue a distance of five hundred miles in little more than thirty-six hours!

Undoubtedly, a traveler will be able to go from Baltimore to New York by the light of a summer's sun when the locomotives shall be placed on the Amboy [New Jersey] railroad. An invitation to a three-o'clock dinner in New York or Philadelphia may now be complied with by the individual who takes his breakfast in either of these cities, and with the locomotive, when established, he may start from one city in the morning and return again in the evening from a visit to the other.

Samuel Breck, member of the Pennsylvania Senate and former member of the United States House of Representatives, journal entry, 1833.

12.   The change described in this excerpt most directly contributed to which of the following?

   A.   The emergence of strong industrial labor unions
   B.   The growth of commerce between the Northeast and the South
   C.   The emergence of new ideas about the proper roles of husbands and wives
   D.   The creation of more interconnected and efficient markers for consumer goods

13.   Based on the excerpt, the author would have most likely supported in the opinion excerpted?

   A.   the goals of the American Colonization Society
   B.   the goals of Clay's American System
   C.   the upsurge in nativist sentiment
   D.   the acquisition of new territories in the West

PROMPT 6

Questions 14 – 16 refer to the excerpt below:

We have met here today to discuss our rights and wrongs, civil and political... We are assembled to protest against a form of government existing without the consent of the governed – to declare our right to be free as man is free, to be represented in the government which we are taxed to support, to have such disgraceful laws as give man the power to take the wages which his wife earns, the property which she inherits, and, in case of separation the children of her love...It is to protest against such unjust laws as these that we are assembled today, and to have them, if possible, forever erased from our statue books...And, strange as it may seem to many, we now demand our right to vote according to the declaration of the government under which we live...The right is ours. Have it, we must. Use it, we will.

Elizabeth Cady Stanton, Seneca Falls Keynote Address, July 19, 1848.

14.   The ideas expressed in the excerpt most directly challenged the early nineteenth century commitment to the ideals of

   A.   limited government.
   B.   *laissez-faire* economics.
   C.   perfectionism.
   D.   republican motherhood.

15.   Which of the following most directly contributed to the problems identified by Elizabeth Cady Stanton in this excerpt?

   A.   The prevailing belief that women should be subordinate to men
   B.   The increased participation of women in factory work
   C.   The rampant spread of middle-class consumerism
   D.   The failure of the Second Great Awakening to achieve meaningful results

16.   One direct long-term effect of the work of Elizabeth Cady Stanton and other women's rights activists was the

   A.   passage of Progressive Era antitrust laws.
   B.   popularity of Flappers during the 1920s.
   C.   ratification of the Nineteenth Amendment.
   D.   expansion of the settlement house movement.

PROMPT 7

Questions 17 – 18 refer to the table below:

YEAR	Percent of Eligible Voter Participation	Percent of States Allowing Voters to Choose Presidential Electors
1812	Not Known	44.4
1816	Not Known	52.6
1820	Not Known	62.5
1824	26.9	75.0
1828	57.6	91.7
1832	55.4	95.8
1836	57.8	95.8
1840	80.2	95.8

17.   Which of the following was a significant cause of the rise of eligible voters from 1824 to 1840?

A.   The rise of mass political parties

B.   The traditional deference given to wealthy elites

C.   The spirit of national unity following the War of 1812

D.   The absence of contentious political issues during the Era of Good Feelings

18.   By 1840, the voting trends depicted in the chart most directly contributed to

A.   reform of the electoral college.

B.   adoption of high protective tariffs.

C.   large-scale European immigration to the United States.

D.   use of conventions to nominate presidential candidates.

PROMPT 8

Questions 19 – 20 refer to the image below:

Unnamed artist, 1832, Courtesy of the Library of Congress

Questions 19 – 20 refer to the previous image:

19. The point of view expressed in this image most directly reflected a reaction to which of the following controversies?

    A.   Jackson's decision to declare war on Mexico
    B.   Jackson's endorsement of the South Carolina Ordinance of Nullification
    C.   Jackson's veto of a bill to reduce tariffs
    D.   Jackson's veto of a bill to recharter the Second Bank of the United States

20. Supporters of Jackson would have most likely argued that he was

    E.   the first president to represent the common man.
    F.   the first president to publicly oppose slavery.
    G.   the first president to endorse Manifest Destiny.
    A.   the first president to encourage immigration from Ireland.

ANSWERS AND EXPLANATIONS

1. (C) The ruling in *McCulloch v. Maryland* established the principle that states cannot interfere with or tax the legitimate activities of the federal government. This established the principle of the supremacy of the national government over the states. Choice D is incorrect because the Court ruled that the federal government has implied powers that go beyond those enumerated in the Constitution.

2. (C) Written by John C. Calhoun, the South Carolina Exposition and Protest argued that a state has the right to nullify, or invalidate, any federal law which that state deems unconstitutional. This directly contradicts the principle of federal supremacy established in *McCulloch v. Maryland*.

3. (B) The decisions in both cases strengthened the power of the national government. *McCulloch v. Maryland* established the primacy of federal jurisdiction in constitutional matters while *Gibbons v. Ogden* gave Congress the power to regulate interstate commerce.

4. (A) Jefferson's 1820 letter is a direct response to the passage of the Missouri Compromise in February 1820. The Tariff of Abominations (1828), the Indian Removal Act (1830), and the Wilmot Proviso (1846) all occurred well after Jefferson's letter.

5. (C) The Missouri Compromise prohibited slavery in the Louisiana Territory north of parallel 36 30' except within the boundaries of the proposed state of Missouri. Answer choice (B) refers to the Northwest Territory. The Northwest Ordinance of 1787 banned slavery in this region.

6. (B) All four answer choices illustrate "the angry passions of men." However, only choice (B) refers to "angry passions" ignited by the issue of slavery in the territories. Choice (D) is incorrect because a "continuous series of slave revolts" did not occur.

7. (D) The Monroe Doctrine was an outgrowth of the principles Adams outlined in this excerpt. As the protector of republican institutions, the United States would not tolerate the creation of new European colonies in the Western Hemisphere. In return, the United States promised it would not interfere with any established European colonies in the Western Hemisphere or in the internal affairs of any European nation.

8. (C) Led by Tecumseh, the Shawnee resisted American incursions onto their tribal lands. Unwilling to respect their independence, Governor William Henry Harrison of the Indiana Territory defeated the Indians in the Battle of Tippecanoe. Choices A, B, and D all reflect the principles identified by Adams.

9. (A) The Senate's opposition to the League of Nations was inspired by America's long-standing tradition of non-interference in European affairs.

10.   (C) The Second Great Awakening inspired an optimistic belief that Americans could improve their own lives by addressing social problems such as promoting better care for the mentally ill, limiting the sale of alcoholic beverages, expanding women's rights, and abolishing slavery.

11.   (D) Many reformers who worked for women's rights were also allied with the campaign to abolish slavery. Choices A, B, and C are incorrect because Southern Redeemers, Populist Party activists, and Republican Party politicians did not exist at the time Garrison published his famous call to abolish slavery.

12.   (D) The excerpt describes an ongoing transportation revolution that promoted the creation of an efficient national economy linking producers and consumers.

13.   (B) Clay's American System called for an aggressive program of internal improvements that would have won the support of the author of this excerpt.

14.   (D) Republican motherhood was the widespread belief that the new American republic offered women the important role of raising their children to be virtuous and responsible citizens. Elizabeth Cady Stanton challenged this important but limited role by advocating a program of sweeping legal reforms that included the right to vote.

15.   (A) The prevailing belief that women should be subordinate to men justified the legal restrictions faced by American women.

16.   (C) The Seneca Falls Convention launched the first great wave of feminist activism. This movement culminated with the passage of the Nineteenth Amendment in 1920.

17.   (A) The emergence of the pro-Jackson Democrats and the anti-Jackson Whigs as mass political parties promoted the dramatic increase in the participation of eligible voters documented in this chart. Choice D is tempting but incorrect. Historians believe that the presence of contentious issues stirred passionate debates that promoted voter participation.

18.   (D) The extension of the suffrage to white male voters led the parties to replace the elitist caucus system with more open and representative nominating conventions.

19.   (D) The artist depicts Jackson as a dangerous monarch who stands before a throne wearing royal robes, holding a scepter, and trampling the Constitution. Although the cartoonist's identity is unknown, the title "King Andrew The First" reflects the point of view of Whigs who denounced Jackson's alleged abuse of presidential power as illustrated by his veto of a bill that would have re-chartered the Second Bank of the United States.

20.   (A) Jackson's supporters argued that Old Hickory was a champion of the common man who rightfully destroyed a bank that favored the rich and powerful.

CHAPTER 5
PERIOD 5
1844 – 1876

Importance: Period 5 generates 10 – 17 percent of the total points on an APUSH exam.

Key Terms: Manifest Destiny, Wilmot Proviso, popular sovereignty, sharecropping, Jim Crow

Key Events: The Mexican-American War, Compromise of 1850, Election of 1860 and Secession, Civil War, Reconstruction, and the Failure of Reconstruction

Additional Resources: See Chapter 5 in the 2023 edition of **Fast Review** for a concise survey of key developments, trends, and patterns in Period 5.

PROMPT 1

Questions 1 - 3 refer to the excerpt below:

But sir, the issue now presented is not whether slavery shall exist unmolested where it now is, but whether it shall be carried to new and distant regions, now free, where the footprint of a slave cannot be found. This, sir, is the issue. Upon it I take my stand and from it I cannot be frightened or driven by idle charges of abolitionism. I ask not that slavery be abolished. I demand that this government preserve the integrity of free territory against the aggressions of slavery – against its wrongful usurpations.

David Wilmot, Representative from Pennsylvania, speech given on February 8, 1847

1. Which of the following would most likely have supported the position expressed in the speech at the time it was delivered to the House of Representatives?

   A.   Proponents of racial equality

   B.   Advocates of free soil

   C.   Supporters of immediate abolition

   D.   Supporters of popular sovereignty

2. People who shared the views expressed in the excerpt most likely supported which of the following?

   A.   The admission of California as a free state

   B.   The Dred Scott decision

   C.   The Fugitive Slave Act

   D.   The raid by John Brown on Harper's Ferry

3. The excerpt can best be understood within the context of which of the following developments?

   A.   Growing nativist sentiment against Catholic immigrants

   B.   Emerging reform movements focused on self-improvement

   C.   Growing Southern support for the concept of nullification

   D.   Sectional divisions over free and enslaved labor

PROMPT 2

Questions 4 – 6 refer to the excerpt below:

I now come back to the question, why cannot this Union exist forever, divided into Free and Slave States, as our fathers made it? It can thus exist if each State will carry out the principles upon which our institutions were founded; to wit, the right of each State to do as it pleases, without meddling with its neighbors. Just act upon that great principle, and this Union will not only live forever, but it will extend and expand until it covers the whole continent, and makes this confederacy one grand, ocean-bound Republic.

Stephen A. Douglas, Lincoln-Douglas Debates, 1858

4. Which of the following ideas supported Douglas's vision of an "ocean-bound Republic"?

   A.   Abolitionism
   B.   Perfectionism
   C.   Republicanism
   D.   Manifest Destiny

5. The Kansas-Nebraska Act heightened the sectional crisis because it

   A.   repealed the Fugitive Slave Act.
   B.   made Kansas and Nebraska free states.
   C.   repealed the Missouri Compromise.
   D.   signaled acceptance of the position advanced by the Wilmot Proviso.

6. Both Lincoln and the Republican Party took which of the following stands on Douglas's position on the expansion of slavery into the Western territories?

   A.   Slavery should remain where it existed but should not be allowed to enter the new Western territories
   B.   Residents of the new Western territories could decide on the basis of popular sovereignty whether to have slavery
   C.   The federal government should purchase slaves from their masters and then relocate them to the west coast of Africa
   D.   The federal government should abolish slavery

PROMPT 3

Questions 7 – 9 refer to the excerpt below:

Resolved, That we, the delegated representatives of the Republican electors of the United States in convention assembled…unite in the following declarations:

7. That the new dogma that the Constitution, of its own force, carries slavery into any or all of the territories of the United States, is a dangerous political heresy, at variance with the explicit provisions of that instrument itself, with contemporaneous exposition, and with legislative and judicial precedent; is revolutionary in its tendency, and subversive of the peace and harmony of the country.

8. That the normal condition of all the territory of the United States is that of freedom…we deny the authority of Congress, of a territorial legislature, or any individuals, to give legal existence to slavery in any territory of the United States.

Republican Party platform of 1860

7. The position expressed in Point 7 most directly expressed opposition to the

    A.   Free soil movement.
    B.   rise of anti-immigrant sentiment.
    C.   provisions of the Northwest Ordinance regarding slavery.
    D.   Supreme Court ruling in *Dred Scott v. Sanford*.

8. The ideas expressed in Point 8 most directly challenged the position of those who advocated

    A.   popular sovereignty.
    B.   Manifest Destiny.
    C.   Social Darwinism.
    D.   Populism.

9. The positions taken by the Republican Party most directly provide evidence of

    A.   the continuing belief in the separation of powers.
    B.   the booming internal slave trade.
    C.   the failure of compromise to lessen sectional tensions.
    D.   the growing support for slavery as a positive good.

PROMPT 4

Questions 10 – 12 refer to the excerpt below:

"I have had but one idea for the last three years to present to the American people, and the phraseology in which I clothe it is the old abolitionist phraseology. I am for the "immediate, unconditional, and universal" enfranchisement of the black man, in every state in the Union. Without this, his liberty is a mockery, without this, you might as well almost retain the old name of slavery for his condition; for in fact, if he is not the slave of the individual master, he is the slave of society, and holds his liberty as a privilege, not as a right. He is at the mercy of the mob and has no means of protecting himself."

Frederick Douglass, "What the Black Man Wants," April 1865

10.   The argument expressed in the excerpt most directly contributed to

    A.   passage of the Fifteenth Amendment.
    B.   passage of Jim Crow segregation laws.
    C.   the Great Migration of Southern blacks to cities in the North.
    D.   the waning commitment to reform in the North.

11.   Which of the following groups would have been most likely to support Douglass's argument?

    A.   Southern Democrats
    B.   Radical Republicans
    C.   Supporters of President Johnson
    D.   Advocates of Social Darwinism

12.   Which of the following provides the best evidence in support of the argument in the excerpt?

    A.   The establishment of sharecropping throughout the South
    B.   The rapid industrialization of the New South
    C.   The sudden outbreak of racial riots throughout the South
    D.   The changes in African American voting patterns and office holdings that occurred during Reconstruction

PROMPT 5

Questions 13 – 14 refer to the excerpt below:

All persons born or naturalized in the United States, and subject to the jurisdiction thereof, are citizens of the United States and of the States wherein they reside. No state shall make or enforce any law which shall abridge the privileges or immunities of citizens of the United States; nor shall any State deprive any person of life, liberty, or property, without due process of law, nor deny any person within its jurisdiction the equal protection of the law.

Fourteenth Amendment, 1868

13. Which of the following was a direct consequence of the ratification of the Fourteenth Amendment?

    A. The extension of the suffrage to all women
    B. The protection of the rights guaranteed by the First Amendment
    C. The invalidation of the *Dred Scott v. Sanford* decision
    D. The acceleration of the migration of former slaves to the North

14. One direct long-term effect of the Fourteenth Amendment was that it

    A. refined the meaning of the "necessary and proper" clause.
    B. altered the meaning of the Preamble to the Constitution.
    C. repudiated the Thirteenth Amendment.
    D. served as the basis for successful civil rights court suits in the 1950s and 1960s.

PROMPT 6

Questions 15 – 17 refer to the excerpt below:

Even though Republicans failed in their effort to establish an effective and durable organization in the South, they nevertheless emerged from the era of Reconstruction in a powerful position…,[and] they found a large number of Southern Democrats remarkably easy to work with….The Fourteenth and Fifteenth Amendments, which could have been adopted only under the conditions of radical Reconstruction, make the blunders of that era…dwindle into insignificance.

Kenneth Stampp, historian, *The Era of Reconstruction*, **1865 – 1877, published in 1965**

15.   Which of the following historical developments provides evidence to support Stampp's argument?

   A.   Sharecropping provided a viable route for economic advancement
   B.   The Democratic Party supported newly enfranchised African Americans
   C.   Booming Southern industries opened opportunities for African Americans
   D.   During Reconstruction a number of African American men were elected to local, state, and federal positions

16.   Which of the following groups did NOT benefit from the Fifteenth Amendment?

   A.   American women
   B.   Abolitionists
   C.   Free soil advocates
   D.   Veterans of the Confederate Army

17.   Which of the following could be used to argue against the claims made in the excerpt?

   A.   The rapid recovery of Southern cotton production
   B.   The enactment of Jim Crow laws
   C.   The work of the Freedmen's Bureau
   D.   The completion of the first transcontinental railroad

PROMPT 7

Questions 18 – 20 refer to the image below:

Thomas Nast, "Worse Than Slavery," 1874 Library of Congress

PROMPT 7

Questions 18 – 20 refer to the previous image:

18. Which of the following occurred most directly as a result of developments such as those depicted in the image?

    A. African Americans formed labor unions to improve working conditions

    B. Reformers renewed debates about the role of religion in society

    C. Democratic politicians renounced the poll tax and the grandfather clause

    D. Southern states failed to uphold basic civil rights for minority groups

19. The point of view expressed in the image was most directly influenced by the

    A. ratification of the Fifteenth Amendment.

    B. issuing of the Emancipation Proclamation.

    C. waning commitment of Republicans to press their reform agenda.

    D. growing opposition to the concept of popular sovereignty.

20. Which of the following groups would be most likely to support the perspective presented in the image?

    A. Southern Democrats

    B. Radical Republicans

    C. Border state Whigs

    D. New South industrialists

ANSWERS AND EXPLANATIONS

1. (B) The phrase "preserve the integrity of free territory" clearly establishes Wilmot as an advocate of free speech. Choice C is incorrect because Wilmot categorically states, "I ask not that slavery be abolished."

2. (A) Wilmot and his Free Soil supporters favored the admission of California as a free state. Choice B is incorrect because they would have opposed the Dred Scott ruling that slaves were a constitutionally protected form of property that could be taken into any state or territory.

3. (D) The Mexican War did not give rise to a new era of harmony. Instead, it ignited an increasingly bitter dispute over the extension of slavery into the new western territories.

4. (D) The phrase "ocean-bound Republic" is consistent with the belief that America had a Manifest Destiny to spread its democratic institutions from the Atlantic to the Pacific.

5. (C) Sponsored by Stephen A. Douglas, the Kansas-Nebraska Act broke the uneasy truce between the North and South. Indignant Northern Democrats denounced the act as a violation of the Missouri Compromise's "sacred pledge" to ban slavery in both Kansas and Nebraska.

6. (A) The Republican platform stated that slavery would continue to be protected in the states where it already existed. However, both Lincoln and the Republican Party opposed the expansion of slavery into the western territories.

7. (D) The Supreme Court ruled in *Dred Scott v. Sanford* that slaves were a constitutionally protected form of property that could be taken into a state or territory. Point 7 expresses the Republican Party's opposition to this ruling.

8. (A) According to popular sovereignty, the settlers of a given territory have the sole right to decide whether to allow or forbid slavery. Point 8 expresses the Republican Party's opposition to this principle.

9. (C) The Republican Party platform provides strong evidence of the failure of compromise to bridge the sectional divide over slavery.

10.   (A) The Fifteenth Amendment prohibited states from denying anyone the right to vote because of race.

11.   (B) Radical Republicans wanted to protect the basic rights of the newly freed African Americans. They supported the Fourteenth and Fifteenth amendments.

12.   (D) The Fifteenth Amendment enabled African Americans to exercise political influence for the first time. This produced a temporary change in voting patterns and office holding in the South. For example, over 600 blacks served as state legislators throughout the South.

13.   (C) The Dred Scott decision ruled that neither slaves nor free blacks were citizens in the political community created by the Constitution. The Fourteenth Amendment reversed this ruling by declaring, "All persons born or naturalized in the United States…are citizens of the United States."

14.   (D) The Fourteenth Amendment's "due process" and "equal protection" clauses served as the legal justification for successful civil rights court suits in the 1950s and 1960s. For example, in *Brown v. Board of Education* the Supreme Court ruled that segregated schools violated the "equal protection of the laws" guaranteed by the Fourteenth Amendment.

15.   (D) The Fifteenth Amendment enabled African American men to exercise political influence for the first time. This produced a significant change in voting patterns and office holding in the South. For example, these new voters helped elect 14 blacks to the House of Representatives and 2 to the Senate.

16.   (A) The Fifteenth Amendment left leading women's rights activists feeling outraged and abandoned. For example, both Susan B. Anthony and Elizabeth Cady Stanton opposed passage of the Fifteenth Amendment.

17.   (B) Southern states passed Jim Crow laws designed to establish social, legal, and economic racial segregation.

18. (D) Anonymous Klansmen, allied with White Leagues, burned black homes, schools, and churches and committed hundreds of murders. This reign of terror created a situation Nast called "Worse Than Slavery."

19. (C) The Radical Republicans had long been the driving force behind the program to reconstruct the South. The image reflects Nast's disappointment with the decline of public support for Reconstruction.

20. (B) Radical Republicans would agree with Nast's point of view. In contrast, Southern Democrats and New South industrialists supported Jim Crow laws. Border State Whigs did not exist as an organized political party.

CHAPTER 6
PERIOD 6
1865 – 1898

Importance: Period 6 generates 10 – 17 percent of the total points on an APUSH exam.

Key Terms: New South, laissez-faire economics, Social Darwinism, Social Gospel

Key Events: Westward expansion, the rise of Industrial Capitalism, Labor in the Gilded Age, Reform in the Gilded Age

Additional Resources: See Chapter 6 in the 2023 edition of **Fast Review** for a concise summary of key developments, trends, and patterns in Period 6.

PROMPT 1

Questions 1 - 3 refer to the excerpt below:

During the last decades of the nineteenth century, the American people embarked on a vast social experiment. Three and a half million former slaves, previously excluded from the civil economy, now joined a free working class, itself undergoing a dramatic transformation. The formal ending of slavery in December 1865 specified no particular political, legal, or social status for the freedmen. Even the great constitutional amendments of 1865 – 1870 and the Reconstruction-era civil rights left aspects of blacks' status and circumstances unclear. Throughout the first postbellum generation, the role that former slaves would play in the nation's labor force, their relationship to former masters and to fellow workers, and the place of blacks in the labor movement remained ill-defined and open to sharp and sometimes violent contestation.

Robert H. Zieger, historian, *For Jobs and Freedom: Race and Labor in America Since 1865*, published in 2007

1. Which of the following statements best describes the "dramatic transformation" affecting late nineteenth century American workers?

    A.   A mass migration of workers to growing cities in the Sunbelt
    B.   A dramatic decline in the gap between the rich and the poor
    C.   A new spirit of harmony between workers and management
    D.   A rapidly growing industrial labor force

2. Which of the following statements best describes the status of African American workers during the late nineteenth century?

    A.   African American activists organized a successful civil rights movement
    B.   African Americans left the Republican Party and became a key component in the Democratic Party coalition of voters.
    C.   African American sharecroppers faced limited economic opportunities
    D.   Blacks migrants took advantage of the free-soil movement across the West

3. Which of the following best describes the experience of African Americans in the late nineteenth century labor movement?

    A.   Leaders of the Knights of Labor excluded them from joining their union
    B.   Trade unions organized by whites generally excluded blacks workers
    C.   The AFL banned affiliates that discriminated against workers because of their race or nationality
    D.   African American workers supported the Industrial Workers of the World's goal of a socialist economic system

PROMPT 2

Questions 4 – 5 refer to the excerpt below:

Mr. Spaulding [a white reverend] took hold of my father's arm and said, "Come and sign the treaty." My father pushed him away, and said: "Why do you ask me to sign away my country? It's your business to talk with us about spirit matters, and not to talk to us about parting with our land." Governor Stevens urged my father to sign the treaty, but he refused. "I will not sign your paper," he said; "you go wherever you please, so do I; you are not a child, I am no child; I can think for myself. No man can think for me. I have no other home than this. I will not give it up to any man. My people would have no home. Take away your paper. I will not touch it with my hand."

Chief Joseph, "An Indian's View of Indian Affairs,"
North American Review, 1879

4. The excerpt best reflects which of the following patterns?

   A. The long-standing desire to expand Protestant Christianity
   B. The long-standing tension caused by conflicting views of property
   C. The long-standing belief in American exceptionalism
   D. The long-standing tension with Canada over the northern border of the United States

5. Interactions such as the one described in this excerpt typically led to

   A. the formation of strong, independent American Indian nations.
   B. legislation that facilitated the equitable distribution of western land.
   C. broken treaties and further incursions onto Indian tribal lands.
   D. Supreme Court decisions upholding the sovereignty of American Indian nations.

PROMPT 3

Questions 6 - 8 refer to the excerpt below:

Mr. President, colored citizens of this country in general, and Chicago in particular, desire to respectfully urge that some action be taken by you as chief magistrate of this great nation…For nearly twenty years lynching crimes…have been committed and permitted by this Christian nation. Nowhere in the civilized world save the United States of America do men, possessing all civil and political power, go out in bands of 50 to 5,000 to hunt down, shoot, hang, or burn to death a single individual, unarmed and absolutely powerless. Statistics show that nearly 10,000 American citizens have been lynched in the past twenty years. To our appeals for justice the stereotyped reply has been that the government could not interfere in a state matter.

Ida B. Wells, remarks to President McKinley reported in the Cleveland Gazette, April 9, 1898

6. Which of the following historic developments of the late nineteenth century most directly caused the situation described in this excerpt?

   A. The emergence of sharecropping as the dominant labor system in the South
   B. The legal sanction given to segregation by the Supreme Court's decision in Plessy v. Ferguson.
   C. The commitment of New South leaders to promote industrialization
   D. Widespread nonviolent marches to protest racial discrimination

7. The situation described in this excerpt most directly contributed to

   A. the Great Migration to cities in the North and Midwest.
   B. using imperialism as a strategy to distract people from domestic problems.
   C. greater support for a national program of vocational education.
   D. national legislation to suppress and punish the crime of lynching.

8. People who shared the views expressed in this excerpt most likely opposed which of the following?

   A. The expansion of black colleges
   B. The extension of the suffrage to American women
   C. The rise of Redeemer governments in the South
   D. The goals of the Social Gospel movement

PROMPT 4

Questions 9 – 11 refer to the excerpt below:

Assembled on the anniversary of the birthday of the nation…,we seek to restore the government of the Republic to the hands of "the plain people," with which class it originated….We demand a graduated income tax….Transportation being a means of exchange and a public necessity, the government should own and operate the railroads in the interest of the people. The telegraph and telephone, like the post office system, being a necessity for the transmission of news, should be owned and operated by the government in the interest of the people.

People's (Populist) Party platform, adopted in Omaha, Nebraska on July 4, 1892

9. The argument expressed in the excerpt most directly contributed to

    A.   big-city machine politicians.
    B.   debt-ridden farmers.
    C.   captains of industry.
    D.   wealthy Wall Street bankers.

10. The Populist Party emerged as a response to

    A.   the women's suffrage movement.
    B.   the growing strength of labor unions.
    C.   the lack of public support for Carnegie's Gospel of Wealth.
    D.   the impact of falling agricultural prices.

11. The Populist Party most strongly supported

    A.   overseas expansion.
    B.   civil rights for African Americans.
    C.   the settlement house movement.
    D.   strengthened federal regulation of interstate commerce.

PROMPT 5

Questions 12 – 14 refer to the excerpt below:

The old South rested everything on slavery and agriculture, unconscious that these could neither give nor maintain healthy growth. The new South presents a perfect democracy, the oligarchs leading in the popular movement; a social system compact and closely knitted, less splendid on the surface, but stronger at the core; a hundred farms for every plantation, fifty homes for every palace, and a diversified industry that meets complex needs of this complex age. The New South is enamored of her new work. Her soul is stirred with the breath of a new life. The light of a grander day is falling fair on her face. She is thrilling with the consciousness of growing power and prosperity.

Henry Grady, "New South" speech, delivered to the New England Society in New York City, December 21, 1886

12.   The excerpt is best understood in the context of efforts to

A.   integrate industry into the South's postwar economy.
B.   provide federal funds for transcontinental railroads.
C.   encourage the growth of the Populist Party in the South.
D.   encourage Southern industrial workers to join labor unions.

13.   Which of the following directly contributed to the development depicted in the excerpt?

A.   The successful elimination of the sharecropping system of agriculture
B.   The successful expansion of Republican political influence in the South
C.   The successful expansion of a new railroad network across the South
D.   The successful integration European immigrants into Southern society

14.   Which of the following historical developments provides evidence that undermines the claims made in this excerpt?

A.   Cotton, rice, and tobacco played smaller role in the South's economy
B.   The majority of Southern men continued to earn their living in farming
C.   Southern leaders provided growing support to end racial segregation
D.   The ongoing mass migration of Southern blacks to cities in the North and Midwest

PROMPT 6

Questions 15 – 17 refer to the excerpt below:

Be a little careful, please! The hall is dark and you might stumble over the children pitching pennies back there. Not that it would hurt them; kicks and cuffs are their daily diet. They have little else. Here where the hall turns and dives into utter darkness is a step, and another, another. A flight of stairs. You can feel your way, if you cannot see it. Close? Yes! What would you have? All the fresh air that ever enters these stairs comes from the hall-door that is forever slamming, and from the windows of dark bedrooms that in turn receive from the stairs their sole supply of the elements God meant to be free…

Jacob Riis, *How the Other Half Lives*, 1890

15.   Conditions like those described in the excerpt contributed most directly to which of the following?

   A.   Widespread calls for a return to an agrarian nation and society
   B.   Fully funded government urban renewal projects
   C.   Economic instability and recession
   D.   The rise of settlement house and Progressive reform movements

16.   Which of the following justified the conditions described in the excerpt?

   A.   Perfectionism
   B.   Social Darwinism
   C.   Manifest Destiny
   D.   Social Gospel

17.   Which of the following was a direct consequence of the publication of *How the Other Half Lives*?

   A.   The popularity of muckraking journalism
   B.   The enactment of legislation to redistribute wealth
   C.   A strong public consensus to promote immigration
   D.   A groundswell of public support to elect Theodore Roosevelt president

PROMPT 7

Questions 18 – 20 refer to the image below:

Bernhard Gillam, "The Protector of our industries," Puck, February 7, 1883

Library of Congress

PROMPT 7

Questions 18 – 20 refer to the previous image:

18. Which of the following economic theories did some late-nineteenth century leaders use to justify the situation depicted in the image?

   A. *Laissez-faire* economics
   B. Mercantilist economics
   C. Socialist economics
   D. Utopian economics

19. Which of the following directly contributed to the development depicted in the image?

   A. The growing power of labor unions
   B. The growing power of political machines
   C. The growing power of the New South
   D. The growing power of industrial capitalism

20. People who shared the point of view in the image would most likely support which of the following?

   A. The temperance movement
   B. The use of federal troops to break the Pullman Strike
   C. The enactment of effective antitrust laws
   D. The use of government subsidies to support transcontinental railroads

ANSWERS AND EXPLANATIONS

1. **(D)** The Second Industrial Revolution sparked a "dramatic transformation" that led to a rapidly growing industrial labor force. Choices A, B, and C are all historically inaccurate.

2. **(C)** Sharecropping created a system of economic exploitation that trapped African American farmers in a seemingly endless cycle of debt and poverty.

3. **(B)** Trade unions such as the AFL generally excluded African American workers. Choice A is incorrect because the Knights of Labor attempted to unify all working men and women into one national union.

4. **(B)** The pattern of interaction in this excerpt typically caused tension between American settlers and American Indians over land ownership.

5. **(C)** Agreements between the United States government and Indian leaders usually only lasted a short time before being broken by settler incursions onto American Indian reservations.

6. **(B)** The Supreme Court's decision in Plessy v. Ferguson legitimized segregation and racial discrimination. This encouraged white supremacists to use lynching and other forms of violence to intimidate blacks and enforce Jim Crow laws.

7. **(A)** The humiliation of Jim Crow segregation crushed the brief spirit of optimism during the initial years of Reconstruction. Grinding poverty, along with the Ku Klux Klan's relentless campaign of intimidation and violence provided compelling reasons for Southern blacks to begin the Great Migration to cities in the North and Midwest.

8. **(C)** Redeemer were Southern political leaders who claimed to "redeem" or save the South from Republican domination. Redeemers supported a New South based upon diversified economic growth and the maintenance of white supremacy. Ida B. Wells and her supporters would have strongly opposed the racist policies endorsed by Redeemer governments.

9. (B) Debt-ridden farmers saw themselves as victims of an unjust system that penalized them with low crop prices and predatory railroad rates while at the same time rewarding Wall Street bankers with extravagant profits.

10.   (D) American farmers faced a prolonged period of falling farm prices. As a result, farmers lacked the financial resources to repay their loans.

11.   (D) The Populist platform called for government control of the railroads.

12.   (A) Grady called for a "New South" that would be home to thriving cities, bustling factories, and rewarding business opportunities. He inspired a generation of Southern leaders who hoped to integrate industry into the South's postwar economy.

13.   (C) Railroads played a key role in the South's economic recovery. By 1900, about 40,000 miles of railroad networked the South – nearly four times the amount of Southern track in 1860.

14.   (B) Despite pockets of industrial development, Grady's dream of a diversified Southern economy remained elusive. In 1900, two-thirds of all Southern men earned their living in farming.

15.   (D) The squalid conditions described in How the Other Half Lives contributed to the growth of the settlement house and Progressive movements. Choices A, B, and C are all historically incorrect.

16.   (B) Social Darwinism is the belief that there is a natural evolutionary process by which the fittest will survive and prosper. This belief justified the impoverished living conditions described in Riis's book as part of a ruthless but natural struggle in which the fit survive and prosper.

17.   (A) Riis's poignant text and pictures inspired a new generation of journalists. During the early 1900s, popular magazines hired writers to expose corruption and social problems. Known as muckrakers, these investigative reporters expressed the new spirit of Progressive reform.

18.   (A) Late nineteenth century business leaders generally endorsed *laissez-faire* economic policies calling for a limited government role in the economy.

19.   (D) The Second Industrial Revolution led to the growing power and influence of industrial capitalism in the United States economy.

20.   (C) The image reflects the point of view of a reformer who opposed giant trusts that dominated the American economy. People who shared this viewpoint would favor effective antitrust laws.

CHAPTER 7
PERIOD 7
1890 – 1945

Importance: Period 7 generates 10 – 17 percent of the total points on an APUSH exam.

Key Terms: Progressivism, Great Migration, flappers, Harlem Renaissance, Isolationism

Key Events: Philippine Insurrection, Progressive movement, Red Scare, mass production of automobiles, Great Depression, New Deal, march of fascist aggression, World War II mobilization

Additional Resources: See Chapter 7 in the 2023 edition of **Fast Review** for a concise summary of key developments, trends, and patterns in Period 7.

PROMPT 1

Questions 1 – 3 refer to the excerpt below:

God Almighty knows how unjust is the war which the imperial arms have provoked and are maintaining against our unfortunate country! If the honest American patriots could understand the sad truth of this declaration, we are sure they would, without the least delay, stop this unspeakable horror…You destroyed the homes to which you had been welcomed as honored guests, killing thousands of those who had been your allies…. The Spanish government, whose despotic cruelty American Imperialism now imitates, and in some respects surpasses, denied to us many of the liberties which you were already enjoying when, under pretext of oppression, you revolted against British domination…. Do you expect us to surrender - to yield our inalienable rights, our home, our properties, our lives, our future destinies, to the absolute control of the United States?

Emilio Aguinaldo, Letter to the American People, June 1900

1. Aguinaldo's letter was written in the context of

   A.   debates over restricting Chinese immigration to the United States.
   B.   debates in the aftermath of the war with Spain.
   C.   repression of radicals during the Red Scare.
   D.   growing isolationist sentiment in the United States.

2. Based upon the excerpt, Aguinaldo would have most likely supported

   A.   competition with China in opening trade with Japan.
   B.   the naval arms race among European and Pacific powers.
   C.   anti-expansionist groups that advocated Filipino independence.
   D.   the right of the United States to assert control over strategic foreign lands.

3. The ideas expressed in the excerpt challenged America's traditional policy of

   A.   criticizing decolonization in Africa.
   B.   avoiding political entanglements in Europe.
   C.   rejecting the League of Nations.
   D.   supporting national self-determination.

PROMPT 2

Questions 4 – 6 refer to the excerpt below:

While much is said about moneymaking, not enough is said about efficient, self-sacrificing toil of head and hand. Are not all these things worth striving for? The Niagara Movement proposes to gain these ends...If we expect to gain our rights by nerveless acquiescence in wrong, then we expect to do what no other nation ever did. What must we do then? We must complain. Yes, plain, blunt complaint, ceaseless agitation, unfailing exposure of dishonesty and wrong – this is the ancient, unerring way to liberty, and we must follow it.

W.E.B. Du Bois, "The Niagara Movement," 1905

4. The ideas expressed in the excerpt most directly challenged

   A. nativism based upon nationality.
   B. legal segregation based upon race.
   C. denial of voting rights based upon sex.
   D. economic discrimination based upon occupation.

5. Du Bois's ideas were most directly a response to

   A. corrupt urban political bosses.
   B. conditions faced by American Indians living on reservations.
   C. the use of loyalty oaths to suppress dissent.
   D. reformers who advocated accommodation and vocational training.

6. Du Bois's call for "ceaseless agitation" was most consistent with which of the following?

   A. The expansion of voting right during the 1830s
   B. The African American migration from the rural South to the urban North during the 1920s
   C. The Beat Generation critique of American culture during the 1950s
   D. The wave of sit-in demonstrations during the early 1960s

PROMPT 3

Questions 7 - 9 refer to the excerpt below:

We learned early to know the children of hard-driven mothers who went out to work all day, sometimes leaving the little things in the casual care of a neighbor, but often locking them into their tenement rooms. The first three crippled children we encountered in the neighborhood had all been injured while their mothers were at work; one had fallen out of a third-story window, another had been burned, and the third had a curved spine due to the fact that for three years he had been tied all day long to the leg of the kitchen table, only to be released at noon by his older brother who had hastily ran in from a neighboring factory to share his lunch with him…Hull House was thus committed to a day nursery which we sustained for sixteen years first in a little cottage on a side street and then in a building for its use called the Children's House.

Jane Addams, *Twenty Years at Hull House*, **1910**

7. Jane Addams created the Hull House day nursery to address the needs of

    A.   European immigrants.
    B.   Southern sharecroppers.
    C.   American Indians.
    D.   Dust Bowl migrants.

8. The excerpt most directly reflects which of the following trends between 1890 and 1920?

    A.   The ideal that women should promote republican values
    B.   The emergence of monopolies that dominated entire businesses
    C.   The continued impact of Populist Party reforms
    D.   The activities of Progressive reformers

9. The activity described in this excerpt has the most in common with work performed by

    A.   colonial women during the American Revolution.
    B.   women reformers during the Second Great Awakening.
    C.   members of NOW during the 1960s.
    D.   radical feminists during the 1970s.

PROMPT 4

Questions 10 – 12 refer to the excerpt below:

By the 1920s the United States possessed the most prolific production technology the world had ever known…[Henry] Ford's work and the emulation of it by other manufacturers led to the establishment of what could be called an ethos of mass production in America. The creation of this ethos marks a significant moment… Certain segments of American society looked at Ford's and the entire automobile industry's ability to produce large quantities of goods at surprisingly low costs… When they did so they wondered why [other goods] could not be approached precisely the same manner in which Ford approached the automobile.

David A. Hounshell, historian, *From the American System to*
Mass Production, **1984**

10. Which of the following could be used to most directly argue against the development described in this excerpt?

    A. Assembly lines forced workers to perform limited and tedious tasks
    B. Assemble lines raised America's overall standard of living
    C. More attention needed to be given to manufacturing household items
    D. Workers would be healthier if manufacturing took place outside cities

11. Which of the following best reflects a continuation of the process described in the excerpt?

    A. The widespread use of air conditioners in Sun Belt states
    B. The growth of organic farming
    C. The use of robots to automate assembly lines
    D. The growing national concern over industrial pollution

12. The automobile's impact upon American life and culture is most similar to that of

    A. clipper ships in the 1850s.
    B. pony express service in the 1860s.
    C. transcontinental railroads in the 1870s.
    A. bicycles in the 1890s.

PROMPT 5

Questions 13 – 15 refer to the excerpt below:

If we survey the situation of our Nation both at home and abroad, we find many satisfactions; we find some causes for concern. We have emerged from the losses of the Great War and the reconstruction following it with increased virility and strength. From this strength we have contributed to the recovery and progress of the world… Through liberation from widespread poverty we have reached a higher degree of individual freedom than ever before.

Herbert Hoover, Inaugural Address, March 4, 1929

13.   Which of the following historical contexts does the excerpt best reflect?

   A.   The spirit of optimism during the early stages of New Deal reforms
   B.   The spirit of optimism during the Wall Street bull market
   C.   The spirit of optimism following the end of the Red Scare
   D.   The spirit of optimism following passage of the Nineteenth Amendment

14.   Which of the following provided an example of how America contributed to "the recovery and progress of the world."

   A.   The Senate's rejection of the League of Nations
   B.   The Senate's rejection of the Kellogg-Briand Pact
   C.   The implementation of the Dawes Plan
   D.   The passage of the Neutrality Acts

15.   Which of the following underlying economic conditions undermined Hoover's boast that America was "liberated from widespread poverty"?

   A.   America's farmers enjoyed unprecedented prosperity
   B.   A severe drought forced thousands to flee the Great Plains
   C.   A widespread middle-class movement to the suburbs
   D.   The simultaneous occurrence of overproduction by business and underconsumption by consumers

PROMPT 6

Questions 16 – 17 refer to the excerpt below:

It is the fact that the Japanese navy has been reconnoitering the Pacific Coast more or less continually and for a considerable period of time, testing and feeling out the American defenses. It is the fact that communication takes place between the enemy at sea and enemy agents on land. These are facts which we shall ignore or minimize at our peril...The Pacific Coast is officially a combat zone; some part of it may at any moment be a battlefield. Nobody's constitutional rights include the right to reside and do business on a battlefield.

Walter Lippmann, "The Fifth Column," *Los Angeles Times*,
February 13, 1942

16.   The argument advanced in the excerpt most directly supported

    A.   the "Defeat Japan First" military strategy.

    B.   the decision to use the atomic bomb to defeat Japan.

    C.   the imposition of stringent restrictions on Chinese labor.

    D.   the forced relocation of Japanese Americans living on the West Coast.

17.   Which of the following Supreme Court decisions used the arguments presented in this excerpt to justify a controversial decision?

    A.   *Plessy v. Ferguson*

    B.   *McCulloch v. Maryland*

    C.   *Korematsu v. United States*

    D.   *Worcester v. Georgia*

PROMPT 7

Questions 18 – 20 refer to the image below:

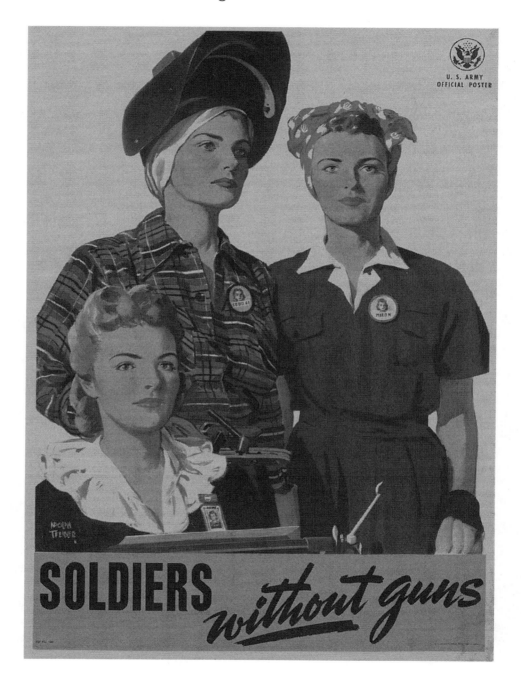

Soldiers without guns, Adolph Treidler, 1944, Library of Congress

PROMPT 7

Questions 18 – 20 refer to the previous image:

18.   The image was most directly intended to

A.   reinforce wartime consumer rationing.

B.   encourage unions to open their membership to women.

C.   launch as second-wave of feminist activism.

D.   convince women that could play an important role in the war effort.

19.   Which of the following represents a later example of the change highlighted in the image?

A.   The revival of the cult of domesticity during the 1950s

B.   The marriage boom following World War II

C.   The equal opportunities provided to women in athletic programs

D.   The campaign to ratify the Equal Rights Amendment

20.   The image best serves as evidence of which of the following wartime trends?

A.   Broadened opportunities for women workers

B.   Enhanced Cold War anxieties

C.   A culture of conformity that emphasized separate spheres for men and women

D.   Popular support for the emerging counterculture

ANSWERS AND EXPLANATIONS

1. **(B)** The McKinley administration ignored evidence that the Filipinos wanted independence. Led by Emilio Aguinaldo, Filipinos resisted American control of their country. Aguinaldo's letter was intended to appeal to antiwar sentiment in the United States.

2. **(C)** Aguinaldo firmly supported American anti-expansionist groups that endorsed Filipino independence.

3. **(D)** Aguinaldo pointed out the contradiction between America's revolutionary ideals and its policy of denying the Filipino people the right to national self-determination.

4. **(B)** Du Bois's ideas directly challenged the system of Jim Crow segregation legitimized by the Supreme Court decision in Plessy v. Ferguson.

5. **(D)** Du Bois opposed Booker T. Washington's policy of accommodation and reliance upon vocational education. Du Bois believed economic success would only be possible if African Americans first won political rights. He therefore advocated a strategy of "ceaseless agitation" and litigation to achieve equal rights.

6. **(D)** Launched by four college students at a Woolworth lunch counter in Greensboro, North Carolina, the sit-in movement represented a clear continuation of Du Bois's call for "ceaseless agitation."

7. **(A)** Jane Addams chose to devote her career to bettering the condition of the urban poor in Chicago. At that time the overwhelming majority of these destitute people were so-called New Immigrants who came from countries in Southern and Eastern Europe.

8. **(D)** Jane Addams was in the forefront of the Progressive movement. Hull House served as a model for other middle-class Progressive women who founded over 400 settlement houses in cities across America.

9. (B) Progressive reformers were inspired by women who worked on behalf of the temperance and abolition movements during the Second Great Awakening.

10.   (A) Critics of the assembly line argued that it reduced workers to human machines who endlessly repeated limited and tedious tasks.

11.   (C) Automobile companies first began to use robots to automate their assembly lines during the 1980s. Manufacturers found that the robots were efficient, cost effective, and safe. These advantages marked a continuation of the automobile assembly lines begun by Henry Ford.

12.   (C) Both the automobile and the transcontinental railroads transformed American life and culture. They both reduced the time it took to travel across the country, thus transforming America from a land of isolated farms and relatively self-contained regions into a mobile, interconnected nation. In addition, both the transcontinental railroads and the automobile stimulated other industries, thus promoting economic growth.

13.   (B) Hoover's optimism reflected the spirit of the Roaring Twenties as the bull market reached its final, frenzied stage.

14.   (C) Financial experts, led by American banker and statesman Charles Dawes, devised a plan to prevent the German economy from collapsing. The Dawes Plan provided an initial $200 million loan from American banks to stabilize the German currency. Implemented in 1924, the Dawes Plan enabled Germany's industrial output to match its prewar level.

15.   (D) The U.S. economy simultaneously experienced overproduction by businesses and underconsumption by consumers. It is important to remember that 60 percent of American families earned less than $2,000 a year. As inventories of unsold goods piled up, stores reduced their orders and factories began to cut back production and lay off workers. These actions set in motion a downward economic spiral.

16.   (D) The final sentence of this excerpt provides conclusive evidence that Walter Lippmann is addressing the issue of Japanese Americans residing on the West Coast. Lippmann's article played an important role in persuading President Roosevelt to issue Executive Order 9066, which allowed the internment of Japanese Americans. Note that Lippmann's article appeared on February 13 and FDR issued Executive Order 9066 on February 19.

17.   (C) The Supreme Court decision in Korematsu v. United States upheld the constitutionality of the Japanese internment. The Court cited the existence of "the gravest imminent danger to public safety."

18.   (D) The image was part of a government campaign to convince American women they could contribute to the war by becoming office workers, welders, and factory workers. Encouraged by slogans such as "Soldiers without guns," about 5 million female workers joined the labor force.

19.   (C) World War II began the process of integrating more and more women into the labor force. Title IX of the Education Amendments of 1972 continued this process of inclusion by ending all-male colleges and providing equal opportunities for women in athletic programs.

20.   (A) The image provides clear evidence of the expanding employment opportunities provided to women workers.

CHAPTER 8
PERIOD 8
1945 – 1980

Importance: Period 8 generates 10 – 17 percent of the total point on an APUSH exam.

Key Terms: Containment, McCarthyism, Domino Theory, Counterculture, Stagflation

Key Events: Cold War, Red Scare, Civil Rights Movement, Vietnam War, Great Society, Youth Culture of the 1960s, Watergate Scandal

Additional Resources: See Chapter 8 in the 2023 edition of **Fast Review** for a concise summary of key developments, trends, and patterns in Period 8.

PROMPT 1

Questions 1 – 3 refer to the excerpt below:

This Treaty [North Atlantic Treaty Organization] is an expression of the desire of the people of the United States for peace and security, for the continuing opportunity to live and work in freedom. Events of this century have taught us that we cannot achieve peace independently. The world has grown too small. The oceans to our east and west no longer protect us from the reach of brutality and aggression… In the last year we have embarked on a great cooperative enterprise with the free nations of Europe to restore the vitality of the European economy…The North Atlantic Treaty is further evidence of our determination to work for a peaceful world.

President Harry S. Truman, Special Message to the Senate Transmitting the North Atlantic Treaty, 1949

1. The concerns expressed in this excerpt emerged most directly from the context of the

   A.   tensions created in the aftermath of the First World War.
   B.   decision to deter communist aggression on the Korean Peninsula.
   C.   outbreak of the Cold War in Europe.
   D.   need to gain access to markets in Eastern Europe.

2. The NATO alliance was intended to

   A.   replace the United Nations.
   B.   support decolonization in Asia and Africa.
   C.   provoke a military confrontation with the Soviet Union.
   D.   deter Soviet expansion.

3. Most historians would argue that Truman's policy marked a departure from

   A.   Washington's policy of avoiding entangling alliances.
   B.   Polk's policy of western expansion in the nineteenth century.
   C.   McKinley's policy of supporting the Cuban revolutionaries.
   D.   Wilson's policy of supporting the League of Nations.

PROMPT 2

Questions 4 – 6 refer to the excerpt below:

Mr. President, I would like to speak briefly and simply about a national condition… The American people are sick and tired of being afraid to speak their minds least they be politically smeared as "Communists" or "Fascists" by their opponents… The American people are sick and tired of seeing innocent people smeared and guilty people whitewashed…As a United States senator, I am not proud of the way in which the Senate has been made a publicity platform for irresponsible sensationalism…As an American, I want to see our nation recapture the strength and unity it once had when we fought the enemy instead of ourselves.

Senator Margaret Chase Smith, Declaration of Conscience, June 1, 1950

4. The excerpt is best understood in the context of

   A.   President Cleveland's use of federal troops to end the Pullman Strike.

   B.   Senator Lodge's efforts to block passage of the League of Nations.

   C.   President Johnson's decision to escalate the Vietnam War.

   D.   Senator McCarthy's campaign to exploit public anxieties about Soviet influence at home and abroad.

5. People who disagreed with the argument expressed in the excerpt would most likely argue that the government should

   A.   remove quotas to restrict immigration from Southern and Eastern Europe.

   B.   increase the power of the National Labor Relations Board.

   C.   monitor and restrict Communist Party activities in the United States.

   D.   curtail Cold War defense spending.

6. The political climate at the time of this excerpt had the most in common with which of the following?

   A.   The attacks on alleged radicals following the First World War

   B.   The isolationist goals of United States foreign policy during the 1930s

   C.   The decline in public confidence and trust in government in the 1970s

   D.   The program to force American Indians to relocate west of the Mississippi River

PROMPT 3

Questions 7 - 9 refer to the excerpt below:

And here's where you come in: to restore valid, meaningful purpose to life in your home...This assignment for you, as wives and mothers, has great advantages. In the first place, it is homework, you can do it in the living room with a baby in your lap or in the kitchen with a can opener in your hand. If you are really clever, maybe you can even practice your saving arts on that unsuspecting man while he's watching television!...Women, especially educated women, have a unique opportunity to influence us, man and boy, and to play a direct part in the unfolding drama of our free society...What you have learned and can learn will fit you for the primary task of making homes and whole human beings in whom rational values of freedom, tolerance, charity, and free inquiry can take root.

Governor Adlai Stevenson, "A Purpose for Modern Woman,"
Commencement Address, Smith College, 1955

7. The view of an educated woman's role presented in this excerpt had the most in common with which of the following?

   A.   The concept of republican motherhood in the 1820s
   B.   The belief in "the white man's burden" in the 1890s
   C.   The image of the flapper in the 1920s
   D.   The image of Rosie the Riveter in the 1940s

8. The excerpt most clearly provides evidence for which of the following?

   A.   The widespread rejection of consumerism and conformity during the 1950s
   B.   The widespread rejection of the beat lifestyle during the 1950s
   C.   The widespread acceptance of Cold War containment during the 1950s
   D.   The widespread acceptance of the cult of domesticity during the 1950s

9. Which of the following most directly undermines Stevenson's argument in the excerpt?

   A.   In 1947, America produced half of the world's manufactured goods, 57 percent of its steel, and 62 percent of its oil
   B.   By 1956, the average age of marriage for men dropped to 22 and to 20 for women
   C.   In 1960, the percentage of married women working outside the home had reached 32 percent, representing 54 percent of all working women
   D.   In 1960, women comprised 85 percent of all librarians, 97 percent of all nurses, and 57 percent of all social workers

PROMPT 4

Questions 10 – 12 refer to the excerpt below:

We regret the decision of the Supreme Court in the school cases as a clear abuse of judicial power…Though there have been no constitutional or acts of Congress changing this established legal principle almost a century old, the Supreme Court of the United States, with no legal basis for such action, undertook to exercise their naked judicial power and substituted their personal and social ideas for the established law of the land. This unwarranted exercise of power by the Court, contrary to the Constitution, is creating chaos and confusion in the States principally affected. It is destroying the amicable relations between the white and Negro races that have been created through 90 years of patient effort by good people of both races. It has planted hatred and suspicion where there has been heretofore friendship and understanding."

The Southern Manifesto, signed by ninety-six Southern members of Congress, March 1956

10. Which of the following was the most immediate result of the Southern Manifesto?

    A. Segregationists in Southern states temporarily closed many public schools in an effort to resist racial integration

    B. Congress adopted new policies designed to round up and prosecute suspected Communists within the United States

    C. The Eisenhower administration experienced a marked decline in public confidence and trust

    D. Dr. King called for a series of "Freedom Rides" to integrate interstate buses

11. The "established legal principle" referred to in the excerpt

    A. defined the Constitution as color-blind.
    B. denounced business combinations in restraint of trade.
    C. sanctioned separate but equal public facilities for African Americans.
    D. declared civil rights legislation unnecessary.

12. Which of the following most directly undermines the Southern Manifesto's contention that Southern whites and blacks enjoyed "amicable relations?"

    A. The Trail of Tears
    B. The Atlanta Compromise
    C. The Harlem Renaissance
    D. The Montgomery Bus Boycott

PROMPT 5

Questions 13 – 15 refer to the excerpt below:

This is a historic occasion...Two years ago your union had not yet won a major victory. Now elections have been held on ranch after ranch and the workers have spoken. They have spoken and they have said, We want a union!...The world must know from this time forward that the migrant farm worker, the Mexican American, is coming into his own right. You are winning a special kind of citizenship; no one is doing it for you – you are winning it yourselves – and therefore no one can ever take it away. And when your children and grandchildren take their place in America – going to high school and college, and taking good jobs at good pay – when you look at them, you will say, "I did this, I was there, at the point of difficulty and danger."

**Senator Robert F. Kennedy, Speech given at
Delores, California, March 10, 1968**

13. The excerpt best reflects which of the following historical developments?

   A. The growing importance of the counterculture
   B. The emergence of a new pro-labor third party
   C. The beginning a conservative resurgence
   D. The rise of organized movements among previously marginalized groups

14. Which of the following most directly contributed to the development described in the excerpt?

   A. The use of nonviolent strikes
   B. The use of court orders to support management
   C. The end of sharecropping in West Coast agriculture
   D. The role of outside political agitators

15. Which of the following represents a continuation of the process described in the excerpt?

   A. The rise of the Sun Belt
   B. The rise of the New Right
   C. The revival of the Ku Klux Klan
   D. The formation of the American Indian Movement (AIM)

PROMPT 6

Questions 16 – 18 refer to the excerpt below:

Policymakers...shared a common...conviction that the United States not only should, but could, control political conditions in South Vietnam, as elsewhere throughout much of the world. This conviction had led Washington to intervene progressively deeper in South Vietnam affairs over the years...This conviction prompted policymakers to escalate the war...Domestic political pressures exerted an equally powerful...influence over the course of U.S. involvement in Vietnam.

Brian VanDeMark, historian, *Into the Quagmire*, **1995**

16. Which of the following was a shared "common conviction" that led to America's involvement in South Vietnam?

   A.   The importance of free trade
   B.   The importance of decolonization in Asia
   C.   The importance of the domino theory
   D.   The importance of nuclear superiority

17. Which of the following was a "domestic political pressure" that influenced U.S. involvement in Vietnam?

   A.   The specter of McCarthyism
   B.   The fall of South Korea
   C.   The French victory at Dienbienphu
   D.   The assassination of President Kennedy

18. The decision to escalate the war in Vietnam resembled the national debate following the

   A.   Wall Street Crash.
   B.   Berlin Blockade.
   C.   Cuban Missile Crisis.
   D.   Spanish-American War.

PROMPT 7

Questions 19 – 20 refer to the excerpt below:

The oath that I have taken is the same oath that was taken by George Washington and by every President under the Constitution. But I assume the Presidency under extraordinary circumstances never before experienced by Americans. This is the hour of history that troubles our minds and hurts our hearts…

I believe that truth is the glue that holds government together, not only our Government but civilization itself. That bond, though strained, is unbroken at home and abroad,

In all my public and private acts as your President, I expect to follow my instincts of openness and candor with full confidence that honesty is always the best policy in the end. My fellow Americans, our long national nightmare is over.

President Gerald Ford, Remarks on Taking the Oath of Office, 1974

19.   Which "long mutual nightmare" is President Ford referencing?

   A.   The shooting at Kent State
   B.   The fall of Saigon
   C.   The OPEC oil embargo
   D.   The Watergate scandal

20.   Which of the following most directly caused the decline of public confidence in the U.S. government during the 1970s?

   A.   The combined effects of stagflation and inflation
   B.   The rise of the conservative movement
   C.   The failure of the counterculture to change business practices
   D.   The influence of computers and the Internet

ANSWERS AND EXPLANATIONS

1. (C) The Truman Doctrine marked the beginning of the Cold War in Europe. The United States pledged to use its strength to contain the spread of communism. The NATO alliance represented an important part of the United States policy of containment.

2. (D) Article 5 of the North Atlantic Treaty commits each member state to consider an attack against one member state to be an attack against them all. The NATO alliance was thus a key part of the US strategy to deter Soviet expansion.

3. (A) The US commitment to defend the nations of Western Europe marked a departure from Washington's Farewell Address advice to avoid entangling alliances.

4. (D) Senator Smith's speech is best understood as a principled response to Senator McCarthy's campaign of innuendo and half-truths.

5. (C) Supporters of Senator McCarthy argued for policies intended to uncover possible communists within the United States.

6. (A) The political climate in the early 1950s resembled the political climate during the First Red Scale following World War I. In both historic periods the fear of communist activities at home and abroad led to attacks on alleged domestic radicals.

7. (A) Republican motherhood was the popular 1820s belief that the new American republic offered women the important role of raising children to be virtuous citizens. Stevenson's message to the graduating women at Smith College "to restore valid meaningful purpose to life in your home" is consistent with the purpose of republican motherhood.

8. (D) The cult of domesticity idealized women in their roles as wives and mothers. Popular during the 19th century, this concept was revived in the new post-World War II child-centered suburbs. Delivered in 1955, Stevenson used his commencement address to urge Smith graduates to welcome their "primary task of making homes."

9. (C) Stevenson seems to assume that women will happily accept their role of becoming housewives. His speech ignores the statistical reality presented in Choice C that a significant number of American women were in fact already working outside their homes. Choice D is incorrect because the jobs of librarians, nurses, and social workers were seen as traditional extensions of women's nurturing role.

10. (A) Inspired by the Southern Manifesto, many Southern states launched a campaign of massive resistance that temporarily closed public schools.

11. (C) The 1896 Supreme Court decision in Plessy v. Ferguson established the doctrine of "separate but equal."

12. (D) The Montgomery Bus Boycott undermined the Southern Manifesto's contention that Southern whites and blacks enjoyed "amicable relations."

13. (D) The civil rights movement created a climate of protest that inspired other discontented minority groups. Migrant farm workers were an important part of this drive for rights.

14. (A) Migrant farm workers successfully used nonviolent strikes, protest marches, and buyer boycotts to win the "major victory" lauded by Senator Kennedy.

15. (D) In 1968, a group of young militant Native Americans embraced the concept of "Red Power" for the American Indian Movement (AIM). AIM activists staged protests that represented a continuation of the tactics used by migrant farm workers.

16.   (C) The domino theory refers to the widespread Cold War belief that if one country falls to communism, its neighbors will also be infected and fall to communism. American Cold War hawks predicted that the fall of South Vietnam would lead to the loss of all of Southeast Asia.

17.   (A) McCarthyism created a climate of paranoia and unsubstantiated accusations, leading to charges that President Truman "lost" China. The specter of similar charges created "domestic political pressures" that influenced President Johnson's decision to escalate the Vietnam War.

18.   (D) The Spanish-American War led to a contentious national debate over US involvement in the Philippines. The arguments in this debate resembled those in the debate over escalating the war in Vietnam.

19.   (D) The Watergate scandal forced Richard Nixon to become the first president to resign from office. Ford referenced this scandal when he told the American people, "our long national nightmare is over."

20.   (A) Foreign policy failures in Vietnam and Iran and the Watergate political scandal eroded public confidence in the U.S. government. However, the OPEC oil embargo unleashed a combination of inflation and stagflation that undercut the economy and public confidence in the U.S. government.

CHAPTER 9
PERIOD 9
1980 – PRESENT

Importance: Period 9 generates 4 – 6 percent of the total points on an APUSH exam.

Key Terms: Reaganomics, Sun Belt, Digital Revolution

Key Events: The conservative movement and the rise of Reagan, the end of the Cold War, the digital revolution, migration during the 1990s and 2000s

Additional Resources: See Chapter 9 in the 2023 edition of **Fast Review** for a concise summary of key developments, trends, and patterns in Period 9.

PROMPT 1

Questions 1 – 3 refer to the excerpt below:

It was in suburbs such as Garden Grove, Orange County, {California}...that small groups of middle-class men and women met in their new tract homes, seeking to turn the tide of liberal dominance. Recruiting the like-minded, they organized study groups, opened "Freedom Forum" bookstores, filled the rolls of the John Birch Society, entered school board races, and worked within the Republican Party, all in an urgent struggle to safeguard their particular vision of freedom and the American heritage.

Lisa McGirr, historian, *Suburban Warriors: The Origins of the New American Right,* **2015**

1. The "middle-class men and women" referenced in the excerpt were part of which broader historical movement?

    A.   The emergence of the counterculture

    B.   The rise of radical feminists

    C.   The drive for minority rights

    D.   The growth of the conservative movement

2. The "tide of liberal dominance" refers most directly to

    A.   The enactment of Great Society programs.

    B.   The election of Ronald Reagan as president.

    C.   The fall of South Vietnam.

    D.   The Persian Gulf War.

3. Which of the following ultimately became political allies of the Orange County men and women described in this excerpt?

    A.   Environmental activists in the Pacific Northwest

    B.   Discontented blue-collar workers in the North and Midwest

    C.   Black Power protesters in urban ghettos

    D.   Native American demonstrators in South Dakota

PROMPT 2

Questions 4 – 6 refer to the excerpt below:

In the present crisis, government is not the solution to our problem; government is the problem...In the days ahead, I will propose removing the roadblocks that have slowed our economy and reduced productivity. Steps will be taken aimed at restoring the balance between the various levels of government...It is time to reawaken this industrial giant, to get government back within its means and to lighten our punitive tax burden. And these will be our first priorities, and on these principles there will be no compromise.

Ronald Reagan, First Inaugural Address, January 21, 1981

4. The ideas expressed in this excerpt most directly challenged the New Deal belief that the power of the federal government should be used to

   A. reform the economy and regulate labor conditions.
   B. promote public ownership of the means of production.
   C. redistribute income to the bottom fifth of wage earners.
   D. promote racial integration in public accommodations.

5. The views expressed in this excerpt promoted a series of legislative policies known as the Reagan Revolution that included

   A. cuts in defense spending.
   B. free-trade policies with Eastern Europe and Russia.
   C. comprehensive national health insurance.
   D. tax cuts to encourage private investment.

6. One direct long-term effect of Reagan's domestic policies was

   A. the expansion of programs to revitalize inner cities.
   B. the growth of the national debt.
   C. the expansion of social welfare programs.
   D. the enactment of stringent environmental regulations.

PROMPT 3

Questions 7 - 9 refer to the excerpt below:

We welcome change and openness; for we believe that freedom and security go together, that the advance of human liberty can only strengthen the cause of world peace…General Secretary Gorbachev, if you seek peace, if you seek prosperity, for the Soviet Union and Eastern Europe, if you seek liberalization: Come here to this gate! Mr. Gorbachev, open this gate! Mr. Gorbachev, Mr. Gorbachev, tear down this wall!

President Ronald Reagan, speech at the Brandenburg Gate in Berlin, Germany, June 12, 1987

7. Which of the following contexts most directly shaped the conditions at the time President Reagan made this speech?

   A.   Gorbachev's ongoing policies of glasnost and perestroika
   B.   Gorbachev's preoccupation with invading Afghanistan
   C.   Gorbachev's preoccupation with containing China
   D.   Gorbachev's pursuit of global free trade agreements

8. President Reagan's speech best reflects a continuation of President Truman's policy of

   A.   reducing American defense spending.
   B.   protecting American interests in the Middle East.
   C.   containing communist ideological influence.
   D.   using the Star Wars missile defense system to deter Soviet aggression.

9. Which of the following occurred most directly as a result of the developments set in motion by President Reagan's speech?

   A.   The fragmentation of NATO
   B.   The spread of communist influence to Latin America
   C.   The withdrawal of U.S. military forces from Vietnam
   D.   The reunification of Germany

PROMPT 4

Questions 10 – 12 refer to the excerpt below:

By the end of the Clinton administration it was clear that U.S. foreign policy had no overarching framework as it did during the Cold War. Rather, each of the two immediate post-Cold War presidents, George H.W. Bush and Bill Clinton, was unsure how to address the emergence of ethnic conflicts and civil wars and humanitarian and human rights crises that accompany them. The result was the emergence of policies that were inconsistent and often opaque.

Joyce P. Kaufman, political scientist, *A Concise History of U.S. Foreign Policy*, **fifth edition 2021**

10. Which strategy provided the "overarching framework" for U.S. foreign policy during the Cold War?

   A. Détente
   B. Isolationism
   C. Containment
   D. Brinksmanship

11. What was an example of an ethnic conflict that occurred during the Clinton administration?

   A. The Persian Gulf War
   B. The Balkan Crisis
   C. The Oslo Accords
   D. The 9/11 Attacks

12. Which of the following best reflects a continuation of the foreign policy process identified in the excerpt?

   A. American presidents responded to the most pressing crisis or conflict
   B. American presidents formed a new system of alliances
   C. American presidents used an enlarged nuclear arsenal to contain China
   D. American presidents focused on reducing global warming

PROMPT 5

Questions 13 – 14 refer to the excerpt below:

On September the 11th, enemies of freedom committed an act of war against our country...Who attacked our country? The evidence we have gathered all points to a collection of loosely affiliated terrorist organizations known as al Qaeda...Our war on terror begins with al Qaeda, but it does not end there. It will not end until every terrorist group of global reach has been found, stopped, and defeated... Every nation, in every region, now has a decision to make. Either you are with us, or you are with the terrorists. From this day forward, any nation that continues to harbor or support terrorism will be regarded by the United State as a hostile regime.

President George W. Bush, Address to the Nation, September 20, 2001

13. Evidence in the excerpt can be used to support which of the following developments in American foreign policy?

    A. A continued stress on deterrence and containment
    B. A return to self-interest and imperialism
    C. A new emphasis on prevention and unilateral action
    D. A return to nonintervention and isolationism

14. The war on terror led America to launch attacks on

    A. Iran and North Korea.
    B. Afghanistan and Iraq.
    C. Iraq and Iran.
    D. Serbia and Pakistan.

PROMPT 6

Questions 15 – 17 refer to the graph below:

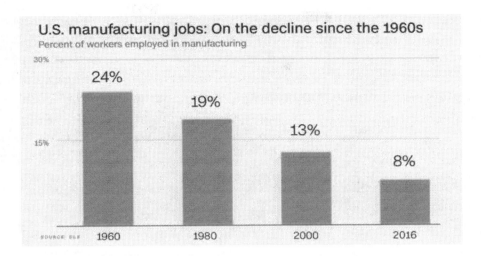

United States Bureau of Labor Statistics

15.   The overall trend from 1960 to 2016 depicted on the graph was most directly caused by the

A.   end of the Cold War.
B.   impact of federal tax cuts.
C.   increasing integration of female workers into the U.S. labor force.
D.   increasing integration of the United States into the world economy.

16.   The overall trend from 1960 to 2016 depicted in the graph most directly led to a decline in

A.   union membership.
B.   Social Security payments.
C.   global trade.
D.   environmental activism.

17.   The overall trend from 1960 to 2016 depicted in the graph contributed to

A.   intense cultural debates over gender roles.
B.   an increase in digital communications.
C.   expansion of the war on terrorism.
D.   wage stagnation and growing income inequality.

PROMPT 7

Questions 18 – 20 refer to the excerpt below:

Today, millions of transistors, each costing far less than a staple, can be etched on wafers of silicon. On these microchips, all the world's information and entertainment can be stored in digital form, processed and zapped to every nook of a networked planet...The microchip has become – like the steam engine, electricity, and the assembly line – an advance that propels a new economy.

**Walter Isaacson, historian and biographer, TIME Magazine,
December 29, 1997**

18.   Which of the following earlier trends was most similar to the transformation described in the excerpt?

A.   The reforms implemented by Radical Reconstruction
B.   The development of national political parties during the 1830s
C.   The Second Industrial Revolution following the Civil War
D.   The attacks on labor activists during the First Red Scare

19.   The excerpt most directly reflects which of the following trends in the 1980s and 1990s?

A.   The expanding political participation of Christian groups
B.   The growing impact of the digital revolution
C.   The deregulation of industry
D.   The continuing cost of Great Society welfare programs

20.   The development described in the excerpt most directly contributed to

A.   the end of the Cold War.
B.   greater attention to industrial pollution.
C.   increased participation in global trade.
D.   growing diversity of the American population.

ANSWERS AND EXPLANATIONS

1.(D) Middle-class men and women living in Sun Belt communities such as Garden Grove formed a key part of the conservative movement that helped elect Ronald Reagan president in 1980.

2.(A) The Great Society, environmental activism, and Supreme Court decisions banning school prayer were all part of the "tide of liberal dominance" that prevailed during most of the 1960s.

3.(B) The conservative coalition ultimately included discontented blue-collar workers known as "Reagan Democrats." Environmental activists, Black Power protesters, and Native American demonstrators did not support the conservative agenda pioneered by the Orange County conservatives described in this excerpt.

4.(A) New Deal Democrats rejected laissez-faire government policies. Instead, they wanted government to play an active role in public life. Reagan challenged this view by calling for reduced government funding for social and welfare programs.

5.(D) Reagan called upon Congress to enact a three-year 25 percent cut in personal and corporate tax rates. He believed these tax cuts would stimulate economic growth. Reporters promptly labeled his economic program "Reaganomics."

6.(B) Reagan's confidence proved to be justified as America enjoyed a sustained economic boom from 1982 to 1988. However, the combination of tax cuts and massive defense spending caused the national debt to triple.

7.(A) In 1986, Gorbachev introduced policies known as glasnost and perestroika. Glasnost, or openness, encouraged Soviet citizens to discuss ways to revitalize their society. Perestroika, or restructuring, encouraged Soviet citizens to revitalize their economy. These two policies formed the context for President Reagan's statement, "If you seek liberalization: Come here to this gate!"

8.(C) Both Truman and Reagan pursued policies designed to restrain communist military power and ideological influence. Calling upon Gorbachev to "tear down this wall" would remove the symbol of the Cold War and thus reduce Soviet ideological influence.

9.(D) The Berlin Wall fell on November 9, 1989, two years after Reagan's speech. The fall of the Berlin Wall led to the reunification of Germany in 1991.

10.   (C) Advanced by George Kennan and adopted as the Truman Doctrine, containment provided the "overarching framework" for U.S. foreign policy during the Cold War.

11.   (B) Clinton was the first American president since Truman who did not have to face Cold War tensions with the Soviet Union. However, ethnic conflicts in the Balkans tested American diplomacy.

12.   (A) Lacking an overarching foreign policy, American presidents responded in a piecemeal basis to each pressing crisis or conflict.

13.   (B) President Bush's war on terror committed the United States to undertake unilateral actions to prevent terrorist organizations from attacking America.

14.   (B) The war on terror led America to launch attacks on Afghanistan and Iraq.

15.   (D) Globalization is the process by which the world's economies are becoming more integrated and interdependent. Globalization has intensified worldwide competition for low-cost sources of labor. As a result, the United States has experienced a steady loss of manufacturing jobs to Mexico and China.

16.   (A) The loss of manufacturing jobs led to a decline in union membership and caused unions difficulties in negotiating for higher wages.

17.   (D) The loss of manufacturing jobs and the decline in union membership have led to wage stagnation among middle-class and working-class families. Between 1980 and 2012 middle-class incomes stagnated while the share of aggregate income earned by the lowest fifth of the population fell from 4.2 percent to 3.2 percent.

18.   (C) The years following the Civil War witnessed the birth of a transformational wave of inventions called the Second Industrial Revolution. Much like microchips in the 1990s, these inventions created new industries that transformed American life.

19.   (B) The excerpt identifies the digital revolution as a powerful trend reshaping American life.

20.   (C) The digital revolution dramatically accelerated the global movement of goods, ideas, and investment capital.

CHAPTER 10
PRACTICE TEST

PROMPT 1

Questions 1 – 3 refer to the excerpt below:

The coming of the American Revolution…created new opportunities for women to participate in politics. Responding to men's appeals, women engaged in a variety of actions in support of the revolutionary cause, which led women to experience a greater sense of connection to and involvement with the polity. After the war their political contributions were praised, celebrated, and remembered…Women now were seen as political beings who had the capacity to influence the course of war, politics, and history.

Rosemarie Zagarri, historian, *Revolutionary Backlash: Women and Politics in the Early American Republic*, **published in 2007**

1. Which of the following best illustrates one of the "new opportunities" open for women during the Revolutionary War?

    A.   Working in textile mills
    B.   Participating in abolition societies
    C.   Creating temperance societies
    D.   Enforcing nonimportation boycotts

2. Which of the following most directly contradicts the argument expressed in the excerpt?

    A.   Women were allowed to fight in the Continental Army
    B.   Women were excluded from political decision-making following the American Revolution
    C.   The idea of republican motherhood enabled women to participate in both the domestic and public spheres
    D.   Women gained important legal and property rights during the Revolutionary War

3. Which of the following best reflects a continuation of the process described in the excerpt?

    A.   The participation of women in frontier mining towns in the Old West
    B.   The participation of women in jazz bands during the Roaring Twenties
    C.   The participation of women in munition plants during World War II
    D.   The participation of women in middle-class suburbs following World War II

PROMPT 2

Questions 4 – 6 refer to the excerpt below:

Here [in 1914] was a congestion the like of which I had never seen before. Within the narrow limits of one-half square mile were crowded together thirty-five thousand people, living tier upon tier, huddled together until the very heavens seemed to be shut out. These narrow alley-like streets of Old Boston were one mass of litter. The air was laden with soot and dirt. Ill odors arose from every direction. Here were no trees; no parks worthy of the name; no playgrounds other than dirty streets for the children to play on; no birds to sing their songs; no flowers to waft their perfume; and only small strips of sky to be seen; while around the entire neighborhood like a mighty cordon, a thousand wheels of commercial activity whirled incessantly day and night, making noises which would rack the sturdiest of nerves.

Constantine M. Panunzio, *The Soul of an Immigrant,* **1923**

4. The conditions described in the excerpt are best understood as a result of which of the following historical developments?

    A.   The First Red Scare
    B.   Restrictive immigration quotas
    C.   The Great Depression
    D.   The Second Industrial Revolution

5. The conditions described in the excerpt were most directly addressed by

    A.   the rapid growth of labor unions.
    B.   New Deal relief programs.
    C.   settlement house workers.
    D.   the migration of African Americans to cities in the North and Midwest.

6. During the late 19th and early 20th centuries, conditions described in the excerpt most directly promoted the

    A.   growth of political machines.
    B.   growth of the Populist Party.
    C.   widespread movement to suburban neighborhoods.
    D.   consolidation of corporations into trusts.

PROMPT 3

Questions 7 - 9 refer to the excerpt below:

If they dare to come out in the open field and defend the gold standard as a good thing, we will fight them to the uttermost. Having behind us the producing masses of this nation and the world, supported by the commercial interests, the laboring interests, and the toilers everywhere, we will answer their demand for a gold standard by saying to them: You shall not press down upon the brow of labor this crown of thorns; you shall not crucify mankind on a cross of gold.

William Jennings Bryan, speech at the Democratic convention, 1896

7. The excerpt is best understood as a direct response to which of the following developments?

    A.   The Haymarket Square Riot

    B.   The continued exploitation of sharecroppers in the South

    C.   The growing debts of farmers

    D.   The increasing exploitation of western forests

8. Problems associated with the conditions described in this excerpt most directly led to

    A.   the growth of utopian communities.

    B.   the formation of the Populist Party.

    C.   the formation of new labor unions to confront the railroads.

    D.   the enactment of government subsidies to support struggling farmers.

9. The sentiments in this excerpt best reflect

    A.   the growing tensions between rural and urban interests.

    B.   the growing nativist opposition to unrestricted immigration.

    C.   the growing public support for labor unions and collective bargaining.

    D.   the growing efforts by Southern leaders to promote industrial development.

PROMPT 4

Questions 10 – 12 refer to the excerpt below:

We, men and women who hereby constitute ourselves as the National Organization for Women, believe that the time has come for a new movement toward true equality for all women in America, and toward a fully equal partnership of the sexes, as part of the world-wide revolution of human rights now taking place within and beyond our national borders….

In the interests of the human dignity of women, we will protest, and endeavor to change, the false image of women now prevalent in the mass media, and in the texts, ceremonies, laws, and practices of our major social institutions. Such images perpetuate contempt for women by society and by women for themselves….

Statement of Purpose, National Organization for Women (NOW), 1966

10. Which of the following earlier movements also actively promoted ideas about a worldwide revolution of human rights?"

    A. The settlement house movement
    B. The Omaha Platform of the Populist Party
    C. The United Negro Improvement Association (UNIA)
    D. The Social Gospel movement

11. During the 1950s and early 1960s, which of the following most directly contributed to the continuation of the "false image of women" fostered by the mass media?

    A. The expansion of middle-class suburban housing developments
    B. The anxieties caused by the Cold War
    C. The shift from a manufacturing to a service economy
    D. The growing feminist protest against the Vietnam War

12. The excerpt best serves as evidence of which of the following trends during the early 1960s?

    A. New technological and scientific advances
    B. Spirit of protest energized by the civil rights movement
    C. New demands for economic rights by Latino Americans
    D. Sharp declines in the number of women in the workforce

PROMPT 5

Questions 13 – 15 refer to the excerpt below:

If we were to offer a symbol of what Harlem has come to mean in the short span of twenty years it would be another statue of liberty on the landward side of New York. It stands for a folk-movement which in human significance can be compared only with the pushing back of the Western frontier in the first half of the last century, or the waves of immigration which have swept in from overseas in the last half. Numerically, far smaller than either of these movements, the volume of migration is such nonetheless that Harlem has become the greatest Negro community the world has known – without counterpart in the South or in Africa. But beyond this, Harlem represents the Negro's latest thrust toward Democracy…In Harlem, Negro life is seizing upon its first chances for group expression and self-determination.

Alain LeRoy Locke, *The New Negro*, **1925**

13.   The ideas expressed in the excerpt most directly contributed to the

A.   New South movement.
B.   Harlem Renaissance.
C.   Square Deal.
D.   New Deal.

14.   The "thrust toward Democracy" referred to in the excerpt was most directly a response to the experience of

A.   nativism.
B.   conspicuous consumption.
C.   nonviolent civil disobedience.
D.   Jim Crow segregation.

15.   The ideas expressed in Locke's essay drew their most significant support from

A.   European immigrants.
B.   big city political bosses.
C.   Great Migration participants.
D.   labor union leaders.

PROMPT 6

Questions 16 – 18 refer to the excerpt below:

We have in the United States history a recurrence of the process of evolution in each western area reached in the process of expansion. Thus American development has exhibited not merely advance along a single line, but a return to primitive conditions on a continually advancing frontier line, and a new development for that area. American social development has been continually beginning over again on the frontier. This perennial rebirth, this fluidity of American life, this expansion westward with its new opportunities, its continuous touch with the simplicity of primitive society, furnish the forces dominating the American character. The true point of view in the history of this nation is not the Atlantic coast, it is the Great West....In this advance, the frontier is the outer edge of the wave – the meeting point between savagery and civilization.

Frederick Jackson Turner, historian, "The Significance of the Frontier in American History," 1893

16.   The excerpt is best understood within the context of

   A.   sectionalism.
   B.   industrialization.
   C.   Manifest Destiny.
   D.   urbanization.

17.   The process described in the excerpt contributed to the

   A.   growth of a widespread consumer culture.
   B.   growth and renewal of American democracy.
   C.   growth of religious revivals.
   D.   growth of environmentalism.

18.   Which of the following could be used to argue against the claims made in the excerpt?

   A.   Western expansion was characterized by conquest and diversity
   B.   Western expansion brought railroads, the telegraph, and other symbols of progress to the frontier states
   C.   Western expansion provided a safety valve for tensions within American society
   D.   Western expansion took place in a largely open and untamed frontier

PROMPT 7

Questions 19 – 21 refer to the excerpt below:

The white race deems itself to be the dominant race in this country...But in view of the Constitution, in the eye of the law, there is in this country no superior, dominant, ruling class of citizens. There is no caste here. Our Constitution is color blind, and neither knows nor tolerates classes among citizens. In respect of civil rights, all citizens are equal before the law. The humblest is the peer of the most powerful. The law regards man as man, and takes no account of his surroundings or his color when his civil rights as guaranteed by the supreme law of the land are involved. It is, therefore, to be regretted that this high tribunal, the final expositor of the fundamental law of the land, has reached the conclusion that it is competent for a State to regulate the enjoyment by citizens of their civil rights solely upon the basis of race.

John Marshall Harlan, dissent in *Plessy v. Ferguson,* **1896**

19.   The *Plessy v. Ferguson* case emerged most directly from the context of which of the following?

   A.   The emergence of militant African American civil rights organizations
   B.   The African American migration from the rural South to the urban North
   C.   The persistence of discrimination based on race
   D.   The nativist resistance to the new immigrants

20.   Which of the following was the most immediate result of the *Plessy v. Ferguson* decision?

   A.   Segregationists in several Southern states temporarily closed many public schools in an effort to resist the decision.
   B.   Sharecropping continued to entrap many black and white tenant farmers in an endless cycle of debt and poverty.
   C.   The "New South" became less dependent upon agriculture and more committed to industrialization.
   D.   Jim Crow segregation laws spread across the South.

21.   Which of the following best represents a continuity with the sentiments expressed by Justice Harlan?

   A.   The Supreme Court decision in *Worcester v. Georgia*
   B.   The Supreme Court decision in *Dred Scott v. Sandford*
   C.   The Supreme Court decision in *Korematsu v. United States*
   D.   The Supreme Court decision in *Brown v. Board of Education*

PROMPT 8

Questions 22 – 24 refer to the graph below:

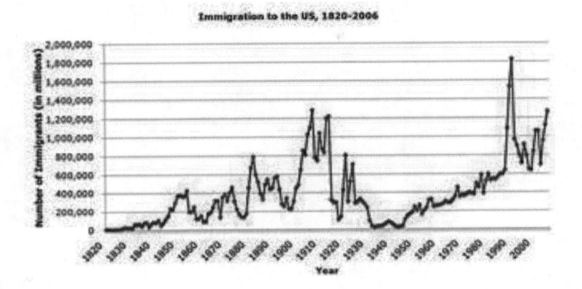

Migration Policy Institute, "Legal Immigration to the United States, 1820 – Present"

PROMPT 8

Questions 22 – 24 refer to the previous graph:

22. Which of the following most directly contributed to the waves of immigration from 1840 to 1860 and from 1890 to 1920?

   A. An American policy encouraging chain migration
   B. Incentives offered to skilled workers
   C. Economic hardships and political oppression in Europe
   D. Fluctuations in American credit and stock markets

23. Which of the following was a direct effect of the waves of immigration from 1840 to 1860 and 1890 – 1920?

   A. An upsurge in nativist activity
   B. A series of protest strikes by American labor unions
   C. The displacement of Native Americans to reservations in the West
   D. The establishment of settlement houses by Progressive reformers

24. Which of the following most directly contributed to the trend depicted in the graph after 1970?

   A. The influence of nativist political parties
   B. Strict regulations on immigrants from Southern and Eastern Europe
   C. A decline in internal migration in the United States
   D. A new immigration system stressing family unification

PROMPT 9

Questions 25 – 27 refer to the excerpt below:

Just the other day, just last Thursday to be exact, one of the finest citizens of Montgomery...was taken from a bus and carried to jail and arrested because she refused to get up to give her seat to a white person....There comes a time when people get tired of being trampled over by the iron feet of oppression....If we are wrong the Supreme Court of this nation is wrong. If we are wrong, the Constitution of the United States is wrong. If we are wrong, God Almighty is wrong....And we are determined here in Montgomery to work and fight until justice runs down like water and righteousness like a mighty stream.

Dr. Martin Luther King, Jr., "Meeting at Holt Street Church,"
December 5, 1955

25. Which of the following developments most directly contributed to the events described in this excerpt?

A. Calls for freedom rides across the South
B. Calls for sit-in demonstrations
C. Calls for a bus boycott
D. Calls for a voter registration drive

26. The excerpt best serves as evidence for which of the following trends during the 1950s?

A. The beginning of demonstrations to oppose nuclear proliferation
B. The beginning of direct-action protests to achieve civil liberties
C. The beginning of a mass movement of people to the suburbs
D. The beginning of beat generation protests against conformity

27. Which of the following occurred most directly as a result of developments described in the excerpt?

A. A complete integration of the U.S. armed forces
B. A Black Power movement emphasizing racial pride
C. A series of protests to end American involvement in Vietnam
D. A nonviolent civil rights movement to remove legal barriers to social and economic inequality

PROMPT 10

Questions 28 – 30 refer to the excerpt below:

This Assembly does explicitly and peremptorily declare that it views the powers of the federal government as resulting from the compact to which the states are parties, as limited by the plain sense and intention of the instrument [the Constitution] constituting that compact, as no further valid than they are authorized by the grants enumerated in that compact; and that, in case of a deliberate, palpable, and dangerous exercise of other powers not granted by the said compact, the states who are parties thereto have the right, and are in duty bound, to interpose for arresting the progress of the evil, and for maintaining within their respective limits, the authorities, rights, and liberties appertaining to them.

James Madison, The Virginia Resolutions, 1798

28. The excerpt was written most directly in response to

A. the XYZ Affair.
B. the ratification of Jay's Treaty.
C. the Alien and Sedition Acts.
D. the federally funded National Road.

29. Which of the following most directly reflects a continuation of the position expressed in the excerpt?

A. The Wilmot Proviso
B. The Trail of Tears
C. The Supreme Court decision in *McCulloch v. Maryland*
D. The South Carolina Exposition and Protest

30. The Virginia Resolution expressed a position about the proper scope of federal powers that led most directly to the ideas of

A. states' rights.
B. Manifest Destiny.
C. nativism.
D. popular sovereignty.

PROMPT 11

Questions 31 – 33 refer to the excerpt below:

The history of life on Earth has been a history of interaction between living things and their surroundings. To a large extent, the physical form and the habits of Earth's vegetation and its animal life have been molded by the environment...The most alarming of all man's assaults upon the environment is the contamination of air, earth, rivers, and sea with dangerous and even lethal [chemical} materials....Our heedless and destructive acts enter into the vast cycles of the Earth and in time will return to bring hazard to ourselves.

Rachel Carson, Silent Spring, 1962

31.   Carson's ideas are most directly a reaction to the

    A.   impact of unparalleled growth upon the environment.
    B.   unforeseen consequences of the Hetch Hetchy Project.
    C.   Success of the national park system.
    D.   Success of Earth Day demonstrations.

32.   Which of the following aspects of Carson's description express a major change in Americans' views of the natural environment?

    A.   The recreational principle that wilderness areas promote tourism
    B.   The aesthetic principle that mountainous scenery is more picturesque than views of the Great Plains
    C.   The preservationist principle that natural wonders should be kept as sources of beauty and inspiration
    D.   The ecological principle that all life is part of an integrated whole

33.   Which of the following later developments best represents an implementation of the ideas presented in the excerpt?

    A.   The construction of the Hoover Dam
    B.   The organization of the Tennessee Valley Authority
    C.   The creation of the Civilian Conservation Corp (CCC)
    D.   The creation of the Environmental Protection Agency (EPA)

PROMPT 12

Questions 34 – 36 refer to the excerpt below:

Little boxes on the hillside,

Little boxes made of ticky tacky

Little boxes on the hillside,

Little boxes all the same…

And the children go to summer camp

And then to the university

Where they are put in boxes

And they come out all the same.

Malvina Reynolds, "Little Boxes," 1962

34.   Which of the following most directly contributed to the point of view expressed in the excerpt?

   A.   A growing belief that urban renewal projects were failing
   B.   A growing concern about the costs of containment
   C.   A growing disillusionment with materialism and conformity
   D.   A growing frustration with programs to end racial injustice

35.   Which of the following groups would have been most likely to support the perspective expressed in the excerpt?

   A.   Conservatives living in the Sun Belt
   B.   Beat writers living in urban enclaves
   C.   Union workers living in the industrial Midwest
   D.   World War II veterans living in Northeastern suburbs

36.   The excerpt can be best understood within the context of which of the following developments?

   A.   The booming post-war economy
   B.   The revived post-war cult of domesticity
   C.   The steady increase in post-war defense spending
   D.   The spreading post-war civil rights movement

PROMPT 13

Questions 37 – 38 refer to the excerpt below:

The day was warm and delightful. From the South Terrace we had a view of Pennsylvania Avenue, crowded with people hurrying towards the Capitol. It was a most exhilarating scene!...We stood on the South steps of the terrace; when the appointed hour came we saw the General and his company advancing up the Avenue, slow, very slow, so impeded was his march by the crowds, thronging around him.....The south side of the Capitol hill was literally alive with the multitude, who stood ready to receive the hero, and the multitude who attended him, "There, there, that is he!" exclaimed different voices. "Which?" asked others. "There is the old man and his gray hair, there is the old veteran, there is Jackson!"...It was the People's day, and the People's President and the People would rule.

Margaret Bayard Smith, eyewitness description of the inauguration of Andrew Jackson, March 4, 1829

37.   Which of the following most directly contributed to the event described in the excerpt?

   A.   The outcome of the nullification crisis
   B.   The expansion of white male suffrage
   C.   The dispute over the Indian Removal Act
   D.   The dispute over the National Bank

38.   Which of the following later developments reflects a continuation of the process described in the excerpt?

   A.   The log cabin and hard cider campaign
   B.   The outpouring of support for the abolition movement
   C.   The insights of Transcendentalist authors
   D.   The popularity of Hudson River School paintings

PROMPT 14

Questions 39 – 41 refer to the excerpt below:

If the end be clearly comprehended within any of the specified powers, and if the measure has an obvious relation to that end, and is not forbidden by any particular provision of the Constitution, it may safely be deemed to come within the compass of the national authority.

Alexander Hamilton, February 23, 1791

39.   Hamilton's views expressed in the excerpt most directly supported which of the following?

  A.   A weak central government
  B.   Opposition toward the French Revolution
  C.   A loose interpretation of the necessary and proper clause
  D.   The addition of a Bill of Rights to the Constitution

40.   Which of the following historical events in the 1790s most directly followed from responses to the argument presented in this excerpt?

  A.   The establishment of the nation's first political parties
  B.   The extension of the suffrage to all white males
  C.   A dispute with Great Britain over the treatment of American loyalists
  D.   Secessionist pressures from influential Southern slaveholders

41.   Which of the following best reflects continuity with the ideas presented in this excerpt?

  A.   Debates over the morality of the internal slave trade
  B.   Debates over the wisdom of women working in textile mills
  C.   Debates over the constitutionality of the American System
  D.   Debates over the consequences of industrial monopolies

PROMPT 15

Questions 42 – 44 refer to the excerpt below:

Europeans began to alter the landscape in ways Native Americans never had. They brought new plants and crops – rice, wheat, barley, oats – and new grasses and weeds, along with fruits such as peaches and oranges. They introduced domesticated animals such as horses, sheep, goats, and pigs, which trampled Indian cornfields and drove away wild game. Their world, quite literally, changed before Indians' eyes as European colonists transformed the forest into farmland… [But] Europe's deadliest export was invisible. Nothing hit Indian societies harder or did more to shape the subsequent course of American history than Old World diseases."

Colin G. Calloway, historian, First Peoples: A Documentary Survey of American Indian History, 2012

42.   The pattern of interaction described by Calloway most directly illustrates which of the following major historical developments in the Atlantic world?

  A.   The origins of the lucrative fur trade
  B.   The origins of the Columbian Exchange
  C.   The origins of the First Great Awakening
  D.   The origins of the trans-Atlantic slave trade

43.   The pattern of interaction described in the excerpt directly led to

  A.   the emergence of food shortages among Native Americans.
  B.   the widespread use of white indentured servants.
  C.   the emergence of a racially mixed population in the English colonies.
  D.   the catastrophic spread of epidemic diseases among Native Americans.

44.   Native American tribes in Virginia and New England responded to the changes described in the excerpt by

  A.   embracing Christianity.
  B.   attempting to assimilate into colonial societies.
  C.   moving to new lands west of the Appalachian Mountains.
  D.   shifting their attitudes from guarded hospitality to open hostility.

PROMPT 16

Questions 45 – 47 refer to the excerpt below:

There is too much hysteria. You know, the world is suffering from a multiplicity of fears. We fear the men in the Kremlin, we fear what they will do to our friends around them; we are fearing what unwise investigators will do to us here at home as they try to combat subversion or bribery or deceit within. We fear depression; we fear the loss of jobs. All of these, with their impact on the human mind, makes us act almost hysterically, and you find the hysterical reactions.

President Dwight Eisenhower, press conference, March 1954

45.   The excerpt can best be understood within the context of which of the following developments?

A.   Cold War tensions with the Soviet Union
B.   Escalating tensions in South Vietnam
C.   Warnings of an impending stock market crash
D.   Deepening concerns about America's declining role in Western Europe

46.   The climate of "hysteria" described in the excerpt is most similar to the climate of fear and anxiety

A.   immediately following the Persian Gulf War.
B.   immediately following World War I.
C.   during the Iran hostage crisis.
D.   during the Watergate scandal.

47.   The phrase "unwise investigators" is a reference to

A.   unsubstantiated claims of financial malfeasance directed at large banks.
B.   deepening concerns about American financial involvement in Latin America.
C.   fears surrounding the emergence of a powerful military-industrial complex.
D.   unsubstantiated claims of disloyalty directed against alleged communist sympathizers.

PROMPT 17

Questions 48 – 50 refer to the excerpt below:

We, the Commissioners of your Majesty's Treasury, beg leave humbly to represent to your Majesty that having taken into consideration the present state of the duties of customs imposed on your Majesty's subjects in America and the West Indies, we find that the revenue arising therefrom is very small and inconsiderable,...and is not yet sufficient to defray a fourth part of the expense necessary for collecting it. We observe with concern that through neglect, connivance, and fraud, not only is revenue impaired, but the commerce of the colonies diverted from its natural course...[This revenue] is more indispensable when the military establishment necessary for maintaining these colonies requires a large revenue to support it, and when their vast increase in territory and population makes the proper regulation of their trade of immediate necessity.

British Order in Council, 1763

48. The Council's recommendation addressed what major concern?

A. The growing colonial protests demanding rights as English subjects
B. The continuing threat posed by French insurrectionists in Canada
C. The lack of American representatives in Parliament
D. The massive national debt caused by the Seven Years' War (French and Indian War)

49. The recommendation in the excerpt most directly led to

A. ending the period of salutary neglect.
B. igniting violent confrontations with outraged colonists.
C. eliminating high tariffs on colonial exports.
D. delegating greater authority to colonial assemblies.

50. How did the colonists initially respond to the new British taxation policies?

A. They formed America's first political parties.
B. They declared independence from Great Britain.
C. They sought an alliance with France.
D. They began boycotts against British goods.

PROMPT 18

Questions 51 – 53 refer to the excerpt below:

Fellow Americans, we are God's chosen people...His power directed Dewey in the East, and He delivered the Spanish fleet into our hands...His great purposes are revealed in the progress of the flag...It is ours to set the world its example of right and honor. We cannot fly from our world duties; it is ours to execute the purpose of a fate that has driven us to be greater than our small intentions. We cannot retreat from any soil where Providence has unfurled our banner; it is ours to save that soil for liberty and civilization. For liberty and civilization and God's promises fulfilled, the flag must henceforth be the symbol and the sign to all mankind.

Albert J. Beveridge, candidate for US Senate from Indiana,
"The March of the Flag" speech, September 16, 1898

51.   The ideas in the excerpt most directly relate to the consequences of the

   A.   Supreme Court decision in *Plessy v. Ferguson*.
   B.   debates over the Wilmot Proviso.
   C.   United States victory in the Spanish-American War.
   D.   debates over the League of Nations.

52.   Evidence in the excerpt can be used to support which of the following claims?

   A.   Beveridge was a champion of containment
   B.   Beveridge was a champion of imperialism
   C.   Beveridge was a champion of isolationism
   D.   Beveridge was a champion of the Good Neighbor Policy

53.   Based upon evidence in the excerpt, it can be inferred that Beveridge would oppose

   A.   big-city political machines.
   B.   immigration quotas for countries in Southern and Eastern Europe.
   C.   an international monetary system based on the gold standard.
   D.   anti-expansionist groups that advocated Filipino independence.

PROMPT 19

Questions 54 – 55 refer to the image below:

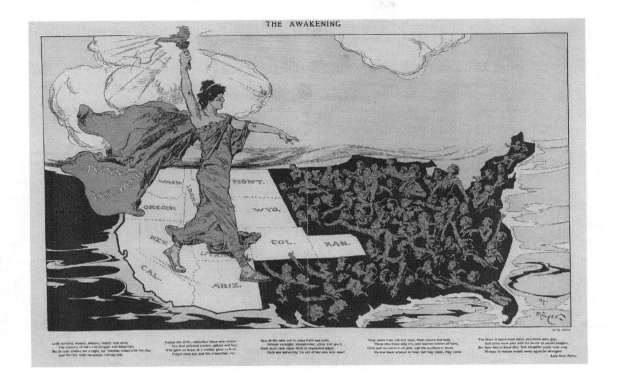

The Awakening, Henry Mayer, February 1915 (The figure is wearing a robe labeled "Votes for Females") Courtesy Library of Congress

PROMPT 19

Questions 54 – 55 refer to the previous image:

54.   The cartoonist most likely supported

   A.   redistribution of wealth.
   B.   women's political equality.
   C.   reform of local government.
   D.   American expansionism.

55.   The sentiments expressed in the image helped persuade Congress to

   A.   enact the Nineteenth Amendment.
   B.   establish restrictive immigration quotas.
   C.   recognize labor's right to form unions and bargain collectively.
   D.   suppress dissent through means such as loyalty oaths.

CHAPTER 11
PRACTICE TEST
ANSWERS AND EXPLANATIONS

ANSWERS AND EXPLANATIONS

PROMPT 1

1.(D) During the Revolutionary War women contributed to the Patriot cause by enforcing nonimportation boycotts of British goods. Choice A, B, and C all incorrect because they occurred after the Revolutionary War.

2.(B) The American Revolution failed to significantly affect women's political rights. For example, women did not participate in the Constitutional Convention. In addition, gender roles for women remained unchanged.

3.(C) The author argues that women experienced a greater sense of "connection and involvement." The participation of women in munition plants during World War II provides a continuation of this process.

PROMPT 2

4.(D) The Second Industrial Revolution created a demand for unskilled labor that attracted waves of immigrants from Southern and Eastern Europe. Many settled in Boston and other East Coast cities.

5.(C) Jane Addams founded Hull House to help Chicago's poorest immigrants. Hull House served as a model for middle-class women who founded over 400 settlement houses in cities across America.

6.(A) Most immigrants were politically inexperienced. Many immigrants became clients of big city political machines. Bosses and ward leaders provided poor immigrants with services such as free food, clothing, and coal in exchange for their votes.

PROMPT 3

7.(C) William Jennings Bryan's "Cross of Gold" speech is a response to the plight of American farmers. Once praised as the backbone of American democracy, farmers now saw themselves as victims of an unjust system that penalized them with low crop prices and predatory railroad rates. Farmers argued that the free and unlimited coinage of silver would bring back their prosperity by increasing the money supply, thereby stimulating inflation and making it easier to repay debts.

8. (B) The wave of agrarian discontent gave birth to the People's or Populist Party.

9. (A) Bryan's speech reflects the growing tension between rural farmers who favored free silver and urban industrialists and workers who supported the gold standard.

PROMPT 4

10. (C) Led by Marcus Garvey, the UNIA argued that the movement for Black advancement in the United States was part of a global process of social change.

11. (A) Middle-class suburbs promoted a revival of the cult of domesticity. Youthful marriages and a soaring birth rate encouraged a return to traditional gender roles in which men pursued careers while women devoted themselves to housework and raising their children.

12. (B) Led by Betty Friedan, the founders of NOW modeled their organization after the NAACP. The Civil Rights movement encouraged a new generation of women activists to demand gender equality.

PROMPT 5

13. (B) The Harlem Renaissance was an outpouring of African American literary and artistic creativity. Locke captured the essence of what black leaders at the time hoped the Harlem Renaissance would be.

14. (D) The "thrust toward Democracy" was an assertion of pride in black individual and group identities. It represented a repudiation of the subordinate status imposed by Jim Crow segregation.

15. (C) The Great Migration was a movement of blacks from the rural South to the urban North. The Harlem Renaissance energized Great Migration participants with a renewed sense of purpose and hope.

PROMPT 6

16.   (C) Manifest Destiny was a nineteenth-century belief that the United States was destined by Providence to spread democratic institutions and liberty from the Atlantic to the Pacific. The ideology of Manifest Destiny provided the context for Turner's frontier thesis.

17.   (D) Turner saw westward expansion as a civilizing force essential to the development of American character and democracy.

18.   (A) Turner's critics view western expansion as characterized by conquest, conflict, and diversity. Western expansion is thus not a positive good, but a series of challenges and uneasy bargains.

PROMPT 7

19.   (C) During the 1890s, Southern states began enacting a number of segregation laws designed to impose a subordinate legal status on their African American citizens. The decision in Plessy v. Ferguson upheld segregation by approving "separate but equal" railroad facilities for African Americans.

20.   (D) The Plessy v. Ferguson decision allowed Jim Crow segregation laws to spread across the South. Within a few years, state and local statues required segregated schools, restaurants, and hotels. Ubiquitous signs mandating "White only" or "Colored" appeared on restroom doors, above water fountains and inside stores.

21.   (D) Justice Harlan's dissent opposed the Supreme Court's decision in Plessy v. Ferguson. In 1954 a unanimous Supreme Court decision in Brown v. Board of Education reversed "separate but equal" schools as a violation of the "equal protection of the laws" guaranteed by the Fourteenth Amendment.

PROMPT 8

22.   (C) Crop failures in Ireland and a failed political revolution in Germany sparked the wave of immigrants from 1840 to 1860. Between 1890 and 1920 a combination of unemployment, crushing poverty, and epidemics of cholera and malaria convinced the so-called New Immigrants from Southern and Eastern Europe to immigrate to America.

23. (A) Both the waves of immigrants from 1840 to 1860 and 1890 to 1920 sparked surges of nativist activity. For example, during the 1850s, the Know-Nothing Party demanded laws that would allow only native-born citizens to hold political offices. The wave of New Immigrants provoked an intense nativist response that led Congress to enact quota laws restricting immigration from Southern and Eastern Europe.

24. (D) The Immigration and Naturalization Act of 1965 abolished the system of national quotas. The law permitted family reunions. By the 1990s, family reunions accounted for two-thirds of all immigrants arriving in America.

PROMPT 9

25. (C) Rosa Parks' refusal to give up her seat and her subsequent arrest sparked calls for a boycott of the Montgomery city buses.

26. (B) The Montgomery Bus Boycott marked the beginning of direct-action protests to achieve civil liberties.

27. (D) Dr. King inspired his followers with a message of nonviolent civil disobedience. He successfully used this strategy in demonstrations throughout the South.

PROMPT 10

28. (C) The Federalists took advantage of the anti-French furor to pass a series of laws known as the Alien and Sedition Acts. Outraged Democratic-Republicans insisted that the real purpose of these acts was to prevent immigrants from voting for their party. Both Jefferson and Madison believed the Alien and Sedition Acts posed a threat to individual liberties caused by unchecked Federalist power.

29. (D) John C. Calhoun drew upon Madison's arguments in the Virginia Resolution to present the doctrine of nullification in the South Carolina Exposition and Protest.

30. (A) By insisting the Union was a compact of sovereign states, the Virginia Resolutions led directly to the ideas supporting states' rights.

PROMPT 11

31.   (A)   Rachel Carson's groundbreaking research convinced her that America's unparalleled growth came with an environmental price. Choice D is tempting, however it is incorrect because Carson published Silent Spring in 1962 and the first Earth Day occurred on April 22, 1970.

32.   (D)   Silent Spring helped launch an environmental movement based upon the ecological principle that all life is part of an integrated web.

33.   (D) Silent Spring and the Earth Day movement helped convince a majority of the American public to demand that the Nixon administration address the nation's pressing environmental problems. The Nixon administration responded by creating the Environmental Protection Agency.

PROMPT 12

34.   (C)   Prevailing cultural beliefs supported conformity and materialism. Reynolds's "Little Boxes" expressed her disillusionment with these values.

35.   (B)   Beat writers in San Francisco and New York City's Greenwich Village were critical of America's "square" lifestyle.

36.   (A)   America's booming post-war economy provided the suburban expansion Reynolds decried in "Little Boxes."

PROMPT 13

37.   (B)   During the 1820s, state legislatures eliminated almost all property qualifications for voting, thus enabling a growing number of white males to vote. The expansion of the electorate provided the context for Jackson's political rise as the champion of the common man.

38.   (A)   The election of William Henry Harrison in 1840 marked the triumph of the new democratic style of running a political campaign. Most historians view the "log cabin and hard cider" campaign of 1840 as the first modern election because both parties actively campaigned among the voting masses.

PROMPT 14

39.   (C) Hamilton favored a "loose" interpretation of the necessary and proper clause, arguing that what the Constitution does not forbid it permits.

40.   (A) Political parties are not mentioned in the Constitution. However, parties began to coalesce around the contrasting economic policies and political views of Alexander Hamilton and Thomas Jefferson.

41.   (C) Sponsored by Henry Clay, the American System called for a national bank to promote economic stability, a tariff to raise revenue, and federally financed international improvements to unite the country. Clay's American System represents a continuation of Hamilton's economic vision. As a result, it sparked a contentious debate over the constitutionality of its proposals.

PROMPT 15

42.   (B) The Columbian Exchange refers to the exchange of plants, animals, germs, and people between the New World and Europe following the discovery of America in 1492. The excerpt identifies many of the key components of this exchange.

43.   (D) The Columbian Exchange included highly contagious and virulent diseases. Smallpox and other Old World diseases decimated the Native American population.

44.   (D) In the beginning, Native Americans in Virginia and New England taught the European colonists how to survive in a new environment. However, Native American leaders soon learned that the colonists represented a threat to their way of life. This led to the outbreak of hostilities in both Virginia and New England.

PROMPT 16

45.   (A) Ongoing Cold War tensions between the United States and the Soviet Union provided the historical context for Eisenhower's statement. Choices B and C are from the wrong time periods. Choice D is an incorrect statement

46.   (B) The climate of hysteria in the early 1950s resembled the climate of fear and paranoia during the First Red Scare following World War I.

47.   (D)   The phrase "unwise investigators" is a reference to Senator McCarthy's campaign to uncover alleged spies who had infiltrated government agencies.

PROMPT 17

48.   (D) The French and Indian War left Great Britain with a great empire and an enormous national debt that doubled to 130 million pounds.

49.   (A) Salutary neglect refers to the lax enforcement of Britain's Navigation Acts. The looming financial crisis forced the King's advisors to recommend a much stricter enforcement of these laws and additional measures to raise revenue from the North American colonies.

50.   (D) The colonies responded to the Stamp Act by calling for a boycott of imported British goods. Choices A, B, and C are all incorrect because they refer to events that occurred well after the Stamp Act.

PROMPT 18

51.   (C) Beveridge's specific references to Dewey victories in the East and to the delivery of the "Spanish fleet into our hands" supports the conclusion that he gave the speech shortly after America's decisive victory in the Spanish-American War.

52.   (B) Beveridge's statement "we cannot retreat from any soil" identifies his ardent support for American imperialism.

53.   D) Beveridge's statement "it is ours to save that soil for liberty and civilization" clearly indicates his opposition to anti-expansionist groups who advocated Filipino independence.

PROMPT 19

54.   (B) The image features a dramatic figure of a torch-bearing female with a flowing robe labeled "Votes for Women." The cartoonist clearly supports the campaign for women's suffrage.

55.   (A) The image shows the figure striding across western states that had already enfranchised their female voters. She is now heading east to states that had not yet enfranchised their female voters. The outstretched arms of women in these states are reaching out to her for support. Five years later, Congress enacted the Nineteenth Amendment giving women the right to vote.

Made in the USA
Middletown, DE
01 May 2023

29821256R00091